IRAN SANCTIONS: IMPACT GOOD OR BAD?

IRAN SANCTIONS: IMPACT GOOD OR BAD?

UNITED STATES GOVERNMENT ACCOUNTABILITY OFFICE

Nova Science Publishers, Inc.
New York

For permission to use material from this book please contact us:
Telephone 631-231-7269; Fax 631-231-8175
Web Site: http://www.novapublishers.com

LIBRARY OF CONGRESS CATALOGING-IN-PUBLICATION DATA

United States. Government Accountability Office.
Iran sanctions : impact good or bad? / GAO.
p. cm.
Includes bibliographical references and index.
ISBN 978-1-60456-551-5 (softcover : alk. paper)
1. Economic sanctions, American--Iran. 2. Iran--Foreign relations--United States. 3. United States--Foreign relations--Iran. 4. Economic sanctions--Iran. 5. United Nations--Sanctions. 6. Nuclear nonproliferation--Iran. 7. Sanctions (International law) I. Title.
KF4678.U55 2008
327.1'17--dc22 2008014429

Published by Nova Science Publishers, Inc. ✣ New York

CONTENTS

PREFACE*

This book describes: (1) U.S. sanctions targeting Iran and their implementation, (2) the reported impact of the sanctions, and (3) factors that affect the ability of U.S. sanctions to reduce Iran's proliferation and terrorism-related activities. This book is an excerpted and indexed edition.

WHY GAO DID THIS STUDY

The 2006 U.S. National Security Strategy stated that the United States faces challenges from Iran, including Iran's proliferation efforts and involvement in international terrorism. To address these concerns, the United States employs a range of tools, including diplomatic pressure, a military presence in the Gulf, and sanctions. A U.S. sanction is a unilateral restriction or condition on economic activity imposed by the United States for reasons of foreign policy or national security.

We were asked to review (1) U.S. sanctions targeting Iran and their implementation, (2) reported sanction impacts, and (3) factors limiting sanctions. To conduct the review, we assessed trade and sanction data, information on Iran's economy and energy sector, and U.S. and international reports on Iran, and discussed sanctions with U.S. officials and Iran experts.

---

* Excerpted from CRS Report GAO-08-58, dated December 2007.

What GAO Recommends

Congress should consider requiring the National Security Council, in collaboration with key agencies, to (1) assess data on Iran sanctions and complete an overall baseline assessment of sanctions, (2) develop a framework for ongoing assessments, and (3) periodically report the results to Congress.

The Department of the Treasury commented that it assesses the impact of financial sanctions. We now cite Treasury's assessments in our report but conclude no overall assessment of all U.S. sanctions has been conducted.

What GAO Found

Since 1987, U.S. agencies have implemented numerous sanctions against Iran. First, Treasury oversees a ban on U.S. trade and investment with Iran and filed over 94 civil penalty cases between 2003 and 2007 against companies violating the prohibition. This ban may be circumvented by shipping U.S. goods to Iran through other countries. Second, State administers laws that sanction foreign parties engaging in proliferation or terrorism-related activities with Iran. Under one law, State has imposed sanctions in 111 instances against Chinese, North Korean, Syrian, and Russian entities. Third, Treasury or State can use financial sanctions to freeze the assets of targeted parties and reduce their access to the U.S. financial system.

U.S. officials report that U.S. sanctions have slowed foreign investment in Iran's petroleum sector, denied parties involved in Iran's proliferation and terrorism activities access to the U.S. financial system, and provided a clear statement of U.S. concerns to the rest of the world. However, other evidence raises questions about the extent of reported impacts. Since 2003, the Iranian government has signed contracts reported at about $20 billion with foreign firms to develop its energy resources. Further, sanctioned Iranian banks may fund their activities in currencies other than the dollar. Moreover, while Iran halted its nuclear weapons program in 2003, according to the November 2007 National Intelligence Estimate, it continues to enrich uranium, acquire advanced weapons technology, and support terrorism. Finally, U.S. agencies do not systematically collect or analyze data demonstrating the overall impact and results of their sanctioning and enforcement actions.

Iran's global trade ties and leading role in energy production make it difficult for the United States to isolate Iran and pressure it to reduce proliferation and support for terrorism. For example, Iran's overall trade with the world has grown since the U.S. imposed sanctions, although this trade has fluctuated. Imports rose sharply following the Iran-Iraq war in 1988 and then declined until 1995; most export growth followed the rise in oil prices beginning in 2002 (see figure). This trade included imports of weapons and nuclear technology. However, multilateral UN sanctions began in December 2006.

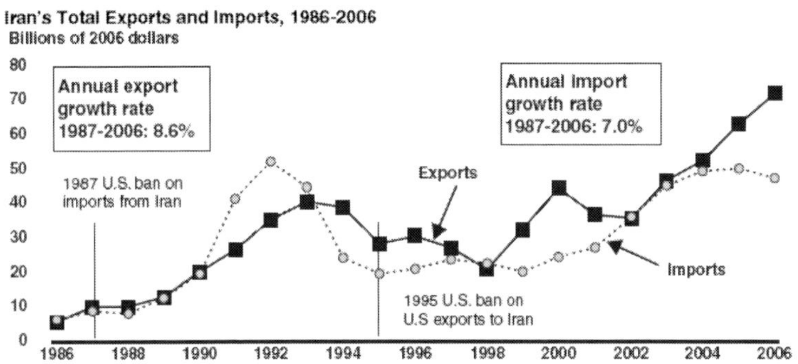

Source: GAO analysis of IMF Direction of Trade Statistics, May 2007.

Abbreviations

BIS	Bureau of Industry and Security (Department of Commerce)
CBP	Customs and Border Protection (Department of Homeland Security
CCL	Commerce Control List
CRS	Congressional Research Service
DHS	Department of Homeland Security
DOD	Department of Defense
EIA	Energy Information Administration
EU	European Union
FBI	Federal Bureau of Investigation (Department of Justice)
GDP	gross domestic product
IAEA	International Atomic Energy Agency
ICE	Immigrations and Customs Enforcement (Department of Homeland Security)
IEEPA	International Emergency Economic Powers Act
ILSA	Iran-Libya Sanctions Act of 1996
IMF	International Monetary Fund
INKSNA	Iran, North Korea, and Syria Nonproliferation Act
INPA	Iran Nonproliferation Act of 2000
ISNA	Iran and Syria Nonproliferation Act
IRGC	Islamic Revolutionary Guard Corps
ITR	Iranian Transaction Regulations
NSC	National Security Council
ODNI	Office of the Director of National Intelligence
OFAC	Office of Foreign Assets Control (Department of the Treasury)
PSV	post-shipment verification

UAE	United Arab Emirates
UN	United Nations
UNSC	United Nations Security Council
WMD	weapons of mass destruction

INTRODUCTION

The 2006 National Security Strategy stated that the challenges that Iran presents to the United States include the country's proliferation efforts, involvement in international terrorism, opposition to the Middle East peace process, and poor human rights record. To address these concerns, the United States employs a range of tools, including diplomacy, a military presence in the Gulf, and unilateral sanctions. The broad U.S. strategy is intended to deter Iran from developing weapons of mass destruction, acquiring advanced conventional weapons, and supporting terrorist activities. Sanctions have played an important role in the U.S. approach to confronting Iran. A U.S. "sanction" is any unilateral restriction or condition on economic activity with respect to a foreign country or foreign entity that is imposed by the United States for reasons of foreign policy or national security.[1]

We reviewed (1) U.S. sanctions targeting Iran and their implementation, (2) the reported impact of the sanctions, and (3) factors that affect the ability of U.S. sanctions to reduce Iran's proliferation and terrorism-related activities.

To determine implementation and assessment of U.S. sanctions involving Iran, we identified and reviewed U.S. executive orders and laws that established sanctions targeted at Iran. While we focused on Iran-specific sanctions, we also reviewed financial sanctions that address proliferation and terrorism concerns that the United States can use against any party, including Iran, as well as United Nations (UN) sanctions. We reviewed data identifying how often sanctions have been imposed. Further, to review assessments and information about sanction impacts and factors influencing sanctions, we reviewed U.S. agency documents and analyzed international trade, energy, and private sector data. We interviewed experts on Iran regarding the sanctions and their impact. We further reviewed documentation from the United Nations, Department of State, and Congressional Research Service (CRS) that identifies current proliferation and terrorism-related activities by Iran. We also reviewed U.S. classified documents related to the imposition of sanctions; however, no classified information is used in this report. On the development of nuclear power and Iran's nuclear program, we reviewed information from the Department of Energy and the International Atomic Energy Agency (IAEA) and the November 2007 National Intelligence Estimate on Iran. For all objectives, we interviewed officials from the Departments of the Treasury, State, Commerce, Defense (DOD), Justice, Homeland Security (DHS), and Energy, as well as the Central Intelligence Agency. We conducted our review from November 2006 to November 2007 in accordance with generally accepted government auditing standards. Appendix I contains a more detailed description of our scope and methodology.

RESULTS IN BRIEF

Since 1987, U.S. agencies have been implementing numerous sanctions against Iran that fall into three categories. First, Treasury leads efforts to implement a comprehensive U.S. trade and investment ban against Iran.[2] Between 2003 and 2007, Treasury filed 94 civil penalty cases against companies violating the ban. However, the ban may be circumvented by exporters who ship U.S. goods to Iran through other countries. Second, State administers sanction laws against foreign parties that engage in proliferation or terrorism-related activities with Iran. State has imposed sanctions under these laws to varying degrees. For example, under one law, sanctions have been imposed in 111 instances. Almost one-half of these cases involved Chinese entities selling sensitive goods to Iran, and over 30 percent of all sanction cases under this law involved parties that were sanctioned multiple times. According to a State official, entities engaged in conventional arms transfers were the most widely sanctioned, followed by those involved in chemical-biological, missile, and nuclear activities. Under another law, sanctions have never been imposed. Third, Treasury or State can designate parties that engage in proliferation or terrorism-related activities involving Iran as subject to financial sanctions that freeze their assets and reduce their access to the U.S. financial system.[3]

U.S. officials and experts report that U.S. sanctions have specific impacts on Iran; however, the extent of such impacts is difficult to determine. First, according to U.S. officials and experts, U.S. sanctions may have slowed foreign investment in Iran's petroleum sector, which hinders Iran's ability to fund its acquisition of prohibited items and terrorism-related activities. Second, U.S. officials state that financial sanctions deny parties involved in Iran's proliferation and terrorism activities access to the U.S. financial system and complicate their support for such activities. For example, in January 2007, the U.S. government sanctioned Bank Sepah as a supporter of the proliferation of weapons of mass destruction, thereby eliminating its access to the U.S. financial system and reducing its ability to conduct dollar transactions. Third, U.S. officials have identified broad impacts of sanctions, such as providing a clear statement of U.S. concerns about Iran. However, other evidence raises questions about the extent of reported economic impacts. Since 2003, the Iranian government has signed contracts reported at approximately $20 billion with foreign firms to develop its energy resources, though it is uncertain whether these contracts will ultimately be carried out. In addition, sanctioned Iranian banks may be able to turn to other financial institutions or fund their activities in currencies other than the U.S. dollar. Moreover, while Iran halted its nuclear weapons program in 2003, according to the November 2007 U.S. National Intelligence Estimate, it continues to acquire advanced weapons components, enrich uranium, and support terrorism. Finally, U.S. agencies do not assess the overall impact of sanctions. Except for Treasury, the agencies, do not collect data demonstrating the direct results of their sanctioning and enforcement actions, such as the types of goods seized under the trade ban or the subsequent actions of sanctioned entities.

Iran's global trade ties and leading role in energy production make it difficult for the United States to isolate Iran and pressure it to reduce proliferation activities and support for terrorism; however, multilateral efforts to target Iran have recently begun. From 1987 through 2006, Iran's exports grew from $8.5 billion to $70 billion, while Iran's imports grew from $7 billion to $46 billion.[4] During that period, the annual real growth rate of Iran's exports was nearly 9 percent and about 7 percent for Iran's imports. Both exports and imports fluctuated during this period. For example, imports rose sharply following the Iran-Iraq war in 1988, and most of Iran's export growth has occurred since 2002, coinciding with sharp increases in oil prices. Iran's trade included imports of weapons and nuclear technology. Second, global interest in purchasing and developing Iran's substantial petroleum reserves has kept Iran active in global commerce. The growing worldwide demand for oil, coupled with high oil prices and Iran's extensive reserves, enabled Iran to generate more than $50 billion in oil revenues in 2006. However, multilateral efforts targeting Iran have recently begun. Beginning in December 2006, and again in March 2007, the UN Security Council (UNSC) adopted sanctions against Iran.[5] Among other things, these sanctions prohibit UN member states from supplying Iran with specific nuclear materials or technology, require them to freeze the financial assets of certain Iranian individuals and companies with ties to Iran's nuclear or ballistic programs, and ban the import of all Iranian conventional arms.

We recommend that the Congress consider requiring the National Security Council (NSC), in collaboration with the Departments of State, the Treasury, Energy, and Commerce; the intelligence community; and U.S. enforcement agencies to (1) collect, analyze, and improve data on Iran sanctions and conduct a baseline assessment of the impact and use of the sanctions; (2) develop a framework for assessing the ongoing impact of U.S. sanctions, taking into consideration the contribution of multilateral sanctions; and (3) report periodically to the Congress on the sanctions' impact.

We provided a draft of this report to the Departments of State, the Treasury, Commerce, Defense, Energy, Justice, and Homeland Security. We also provided a draft to the NSC and the Office of the Director of National Intelligence (ODNI). The Department of the Treasury provided a formal response emphasizing that, as a result of financial pressure, Iran is experiencing increasing isolation from the global community. The department also states that Iran continues to pursue nuclear capabilities and ballistic missile technology and to fund terrorism. This comment reinforces our finding that the overall impact of sanctions is unclear. In addition, Treasury noted its assessments of the effectiveness of financial sanctions. We revised the report to recognize that Treasury assesses the impact of financial sanctions but maintain that an overall impact assessment of all U.S. sanctions has not been undertaken. Treasury's letter can be found in appendix V.

The Departments of State, the Treasury, Commerce, and Energy provided written technical comments. We incorporated these comments into the report as appropriate. The Department of Commerce submitted its technical comments in a letter that is included in appendix VI. The NSC provided brief oral comments and ODNI provided a classified response; we considered this information and revised the report as appropriate. The Departments of Defense, Justice, and Homeland Security provided no comments on the draft report, though Homeland Security supported the part of our Matter for Congressional Consideration that specifically involves the department.

BACKGROUND

Iran is a nation of strategic importance due to its central geographic location and huge reserves of fossil fuels. Iran's neighbors include Iraq and Afghanistan, two countries with ongoing U.S. and coalition military operations, and Pakistan and Turkey, key U.S. allies in the global war on terrorism (see figure 1). Furthermore, Iran borders both the Persian Gulf and the Strait of Hormuz, through which roughly one-fifth of the global oil supply is exported. According to the Department of Energy, Iran has the third largest proven oil reserves in the world. Iran's oil export revenues constitute about 80 percent of its total export revenue, and accounted for nearly one-fifth of its gross domestic product (GDP) in 2004. High oil prices in recent years have further boosted Iran's oil export revenues.

U.S.-Iranian relations have often been strained since the early years of the Cold War. Following the U.S.-supported overthrow of Iran's prime minister in 1953, the United States and others backed the regime of Shah Mohammed Reza Pahlavi for a quarter century. Although it did much to develop the country economically, the Shah's government repressed political dissent. In 1978, domestic turmoil swept the country as a result of religious and political opposition to the Shah's rule, culminating in the collapse of the Shah's government in February 1979 and the establishment of an Islamic republic led by Supreme Leader Ayatollah Khomeini. In November 1979, militant Iranian students occupied the American embassy in Tehran with the support of Khomeini. Shortly thereafter, the United States broke diplomatic relations with Iran, which remain suspended to this day.

Source: GAO.

Figure 1. Map of Iran.

Chapter 1

U.S. AGENCIES IMPLEMENT NUMEROUS SANCTIONS TARGETING IRAN

U.S. sanctions to deter Iran's proliferation and support for terrorism fall into three categories. First, Treasury leads U.S. government efforts to implement a comprehensive trade and investment ban against Iran. Second, State is responsible for implementing several laws that sanction foreign parties engaging in proliferation or terrorism-related transactions with Iran. Third, Treasury or State can impose financial sanctions, including a freeze on assets and a prohibition on access to U.S. financial institutions, against parties who engage in proliferation or terrorism-related activities with any party, including Iran. (See app. II for more information regarding the timing and nature of U.S. and UN sanctions.)

TREASURY'S TRADE AND INVESTMENT BAN PROHIBITS VIRTUALLY ALL U.S. COMMERCIAL TIES WITH IRAN, BUT TRANSSHIPMENTS MAY CIRCUMVENT BAN

Treasury administers a ban on almost all U.S. trade or investment activity involving Iran.[6] The prohibitions of the trade and investment ban began with a 1987 ban on Iranian imports and were followed by a 1995 ban on U.S. exports to and investment in Iran. These prohibitions apply to U.S. persons, including U.S. companies and their foreign branches, wherever located.[7] U.S. officials stated that the ban does not apply to independent foreign subsidiaries of U.S. companies.[8] Non-U.S. persons are generally exempt from the provisions of the ban.[9] Trade sanctions against Iran were eased in 2000 to allow for the purchase and import from Iran of carpets and food products.[10] Further, the Trade Sanctions Reform and Export Enhancement Act of 2000 lifted, subject to certain exceptions, U.S. sanctions on commercial sales of food, agricultural commodities, and medical products to several sanctioned countries, including Iran.[11] The ban also prohibits U.S. financial institutions from having direct banking relationships with banks in Iran and banks owned or controlled by the government of Iran.[12]

According to a Treasury official, the trade and investment ban is aimed at making it more difficult for Iran to procure U.S. goods, services, and technology, including those that could be used for terrorism or proliferation. The official further stated that, as with all U.S. economic sanctions programs, the premise of the sanctions is to exact a price on the sanctioned entity, which serves as an inducement to change the behavior that threatens U.S. national security and foreign policy goals. Sanctions also serve to make it more difficult for a sanctioned entity to pursue its threatening conduct.

Treasury's Office of Foreign Assets Control (OFAC) administers the trade and investment ban and is responsible for reviewing and licensing requests to export or re-export goods to Iran, with most items subject to a general policy of denial. OFAC is also responsible for conducting civil investigations of sanctions violations, which can result in warning letters, cease and desist orders, and civil penalties of up to $250,000 (or an amount that is twice the amount of the transaction that is the basis for the violation) imposed administratively. We found that Iran sanctions were involved in 94 out of 425 civil penalty cases that OFAC assessed or settled as a result of sanction violations between 2003 and 2007. In cases where OFAC finds evidence of willful violations of the trade and investment ban, it may refer those cases to other federal law enforcement agencies for criminal investigation. Investigations of potential criminal violations can be conducted by the Department of Commerce's Bureau of Industry and Security (BIS), DHS's Immigration and Customs Enforcement (ICE), and the Department of Justice's Federal Bureau of Investigation (FBI), sometimes acting jointly. Criminal prosecutions are pursued by the Department of Justice. Under recently enacted legislation, criminal penalties for violations of the trade and investment ban can range up to $1,000,000 and (for natural persons) 20 years in jail.[13]

According to officials at key U.S. export enforcement agencies, the trade ban may be circumvented by the transshipment of U.S. exports through third countries. Officials identified several locations that serve as common transshipment points for goods destined for Iran. These locations include

Germany, Malaysia, Singapore, the United Kingdom, and, according to Commerce officials, the United Arab Emirates (UAE) in particular.

Two trends underscore the possibility that U.S. goods are being shipped to Iran through the UAE. First is the considerable growth in U.S. trade flows through the UAE. The United States has become the number one supplier of imports to the UAE and Iran is the UAE's largest trade partner. Moreover, although trade statistics do not specify the portion of UAE exports to Iran that are of U.S.-origin, the UAE transships a higher proportion of its U.S. imports than other countries do. According to Commerce officials transshipments have been a considerable problem in terms of the effectiveness of sanctions in place against Iran. The second trend is the high rate of unfavorable end-use checks for U.S. items exported to the UAE. The Department of Commerce relies on post-shipment verification (PSV) checks as its primary method of detecting and preventing illegal transfers, including transshipments, of U.S.-origin exports to Iran. However, according to Commerce officials, in August 2007, the UAE enacted a comprehensive export, reexport, and transshipment control law to better enable the UAE to control transshipment of sensitive goods through its ports. The law is too new to assess its effectiveness. (Further information is classified.)

State Sanctions Foreign Entities under Iran-Specific Laws

Congress has taken steps to discourage trade by third-country parties with Iran by enacting sanction laws that have a "secondary boycott" effect. Three U.S. sanction laws discourage foreign parties from engaging in proliferation or terrorism-related activities with Iran (see table 1). State leads efforts to implement these laws and has imposed sanctions under these laws to varying degrees.

Table 1. U.S. Sanction Laws Targeting Iran

U.S. law	Sanctionable activities	Sanctions imposed against foreign parties	Use of sanctions
Iran, North Korea, and Syria Nonproliferation Act[a]	Transfer to Iran of goods, services, or technology listed in various multilateral export control arrangements or that contribute to weapons of mass destruction or missile programs.	Among other things, no U.S. government procurement, no U.S. assistance, no licenses for exports from the United States to the foreign party of defense or dual-use items. *Sanctions are discretionary and State has typically imposed sanctions for a 2-year period.*	Sanctions imposed 111 times since 2000 in Iran- related cases, including: 52 instances against • Chinese parties, • 9 instances against North Korean parties, • 8 instances against Syrian parties, and • 7 instances against Russian parties.
Iran-Iraq Arms Nonproliferation Act of 1992[b]	Transfer to Iran of controlled goods or technology so as to contribute "knowingly and materially" to Iran's efforts to acquire destabilizing numbers and types of advanced conventional weapons.	*Against persons*: No U.S. government procurement or export licenses. *Against foreign countries:* Among other things, no U.S. government assistance or support for multilateral development bank assistance. *Sanctions are mandatory and are imposed for a 2-year period against persons and for a 1-year period against foreign countries.* *The President also has the authority to impose an additional discretionary sanction against foreign countries.*	Sanctions imposed 12 times in 2002 and 2003.

Table 1. (Continued).

U.S. law	Sanctionable activities	Sanctions imposed against foreign parties	Use of sanctions
Iran Sanctions Act[c]	Investment of $20 million or more within a 12-month period that directly and significantly contributed to the enhancement of Iran's ability to develop its petroleum resources. Exports, transfers, or other provision to Iran of any goods, services, technology or other items knowing that the provision of such items would contribute materially to Iran's ability to acquire or develop chemical, biological, or nuclear weapons or related technologies; or destabilizing numbers and types of advanced conventional weapons.	Two of the following options: • no Export-Import Bank assistance, • no export licenses to export certain goods to sanctioned parties, • no loans or credits totaling more than $5 million in a 12- month period from U.S. financial institutions, • no U.S. government procurement, • for sanctioned financial institutions, no designation as a primary dealer in U.S. government debt instruments, and may not serve as an agent of the U.S. government or as repository for U.S. government funds, or • additional sanctions, as appropriate, to restrict imports regarding the sanctioned party. *Sanctions are mandatory and are imposed for a period of not less than 2 years.*	Sanctions never imposed, though State officials note that the law has been used as a tool in diplomatic efforts.

Source: U.S. public laws, http://www.state.gov/t/isn/c15231.htm, Federal Register.

[a] This law was enacted as the Iran Nonproliferation Act of 2000; Restriction on Extraordinary Payments in Connection with the International Space Station, Pub. L. No. 106-178, 114 Stat. 38; Syria was added to the act in 2005 by the Iran Nonproliferation Amendments Act of 2005, Pub. L. No. 109-112, §4, 119 Stat. 2366, 2369; and North Korea was added in 2006 by the North Korea Nonproliferation Act of 2006, Pub. L. No. 109-2353, 120 Stat. 2015.

[b] Enacted by the National Defense Authorization Act for fiscal year 1993, Pub. L. No. 102-484, Title XVI, 106 Stat. 2315, 2571-75 (1992). We are unable to distinguish between Iran and Iraq sanction cases, as this information is classified.

[c] This act was originally enacted as the Iran-Libya Sanctions Act of 1996, Pub. L. No. 104-172, 110 Stat. 1541; Libya was removed from the law in 2006 by the Iran Freedom Support Act, Pub. L. No. 109-293, 120 Stat. 1344. Proliferation-related sanctionable activities were added to the law in 2006.

As table 1 shows, State has imposed sanctions against foreign parties, including bans on U.S. government procurement opportunities and sales of defense-related items, in 111 Iran-specific cases since 2000 under a law currently known as the Iran, North Korea, and Syria Nonproliferation Act (INKSNA).[14] This law targets foreign persons that have transferred goods, services, or technology to Iran that are listed on various multilateral export control lists.[15] According to a State official, entities engaged in conventional arms transfers were the most widely sanctioned, followed by those involved in chemical-biological, missile, and nuclear activities. Since 2000, almost half of the cases (52) involved Chinese parties, with North Korean and Russian parties accounting for 9 and 7 cases, respectively. In 2007, Syrian parties were sanctioned in 8 cases. According to State officials, in most cases, the full range of sanctions authorized under INKSNA is imposed, and sanctions have been typically imposed for a 2-year period. Over 30 percent of all sanction cases involve parties that were sanctioned multiple times under the law—some, primarily Chinese firms, 3 or more times. According to a State official, such instances were the result of new proliferation activities by these firms. Because the law establishes the sanctions that are available, the practical effect of continuing to impose sanctions against the same parties is to extend the length of time the sanctions are imposed and make the public aware of the firms facilitating proliferation with Iran. State officials said that generally no consideration of additional penalties or measures is given to parties who have been sanctioned multiple times, although some of these entities have been sanctioned under other sanction tools. However, State officials emphasized that they raise concerns about the activities of such entities with foreign governments as appropriate.

In deciding to sanction an entity under INKSNA, State officials reported that every 6 months they assess as many as 60,000 intelligence reports to identify transfer cases that should be submitted to agencies for review. State decides, on a discretionary basis, which parties to sanction following a meeting chaired by the NSC that solicits input from DOD, Energy, and Treasury and other agencies regarding the disposition of each case. According to a State official, the Deputy Assistant Secretary-level interagency group reviews cases to recommend whether the foreign persons were reportable under the act, and if so, (1) whether there was information establishing that a case was exempt from sanctions under the act, (2) whether to seek from the foreign person additional information concerning the transfer or acquisition as provided for in the act, and (3) whether sanctions under the act should be applied. The final decision regarding the disposition of each case is made by the Deputy Secretary of State. One State official noted that there have been several cases in which State decided not to impose sanctions because of positive nonproliferation actions taken by the foreign government responsible for the firm engaging in the proliferation transfer. A foreign government punishing or prosecuting the firm responsible for the transfer is one example of the type of positive action that has resulted in a decision not to impose penalties. Another reason why State may decide not to impose sanctions is a concern that such an action, which is made public, may compromise the intelligence "sources and methods" used to collect information on a particular proliferation case. Once final decisions are made, State then submits a classified report to Congress identifying parties that have engaged in sanctionable activities and parties that will be sanctioned, and ultimately publishes the names of sanctioned entities in the *Federal Register*.[16] (See appendix III for a detailed listing of these sanction cases.)

Under a second law, the Iran-Iraq Arms Nonproliferation Act of 1992[17] (also shown in table 1), State has imposed sanctions 12 times. Under this act, mandatory sanctions include prohibiting the export to Iran of all goods specified on the Commerce Control List (CCL).[18] State also can impose sanctions against foreign parties, such as a ban on U.S. government procurement opportunities or export licenses that knowingly and materially contribute to Iran's efforts to acquire destabilizing numbers and types of advanced conventional weapons. As with the Iran, North Korea, and Syria Nonproliferation Act, decisions under this act include interagency input from Commerce, Energy, and DOD, with State in the lead and responsible for deciding which cases warrant imposition of sanctions. In 2002, State imposed sanctions in 10 instances, 9 of which were against Chinese parties.[19] In 2003, sanctions were imposed against two parties, one Jordanian and one Indian. No sanctions have been imposed since 2003 primarily because, according to State officials, it is difficult to establish that transfers were made by parties who knowingly and materially contributed to Iran's proliferation.

Table 1 shows that State has not imposed sanctions against any party under a third law—the Iran Sanctions Act—though State officials noted that the law has been useful in raising U.S. concerns over Iran. The goal of the Iran Sanctions Act (previously known as the Iran-Libya Sanctions Act of 1996,[20] or ILSA) has been to deny Iran the financial resources to support international terrorism or the development of weapons of mass destruction (WMD) by limiting Iran's ability to find, extract, refine, or transport its oil resources. State considered sanctions on one occasion in 1998; however, the

U.S. government granted waivers to the parties involved.[21] In that instance, the U.S. government determined that the investments of three foreign companies—Total (France), Gazprom (Russia), and Petronas (Malaysia)–in the development of Iran's South Pars gas field were sanctionable under ILSA. However, the Secretary of State determined that it was important to the U.S. national interest to waive the imposition of sanctions against these firms. In making this determination, the Secretary considered factors such as the desire to build an effective multilateral regime to deny Iran the ability to acquire WMD and support acts of international terrorism. Further, the European Union (EU) had concerns that the use of the act to impose sanctions would constitute extraterritorial application of U.S. law. The possibility that the EU might take this issue to the World Trade Organization for resolution played a role in convincing the U.S. government to waive sanctions. In addition, a report on the use of ILSA prepared by State and cleared by the NSC noted that the sanctions that could be imposed were unlikely to induce the three companies to abandon their investments because the companies were insulated from any practical negative impact of the sanctions.[22]

Targeted Financial Sanctions Freeze Assets of Parties Involved in Proliferation and Terrorism-Related Activities

The U.S. government has taken actions against Iran using targeted financial sanctions that can be used against any party that engages in certain proliferation or terrorism activities.[23] In June 2005, the President issued Executive Order 13382 to freeze the assets of persons engaged in proliferation of WMD and members of their support networks.[24] This action followed the issuance in September 2001 of Executive Order 13224 to freeze the assets of persons who commit, threaten to commit, or support terrorism.[25] Executive Orders 13382 and 13224 were both issued under the authority of the International Economic Emergency Powers Act (IEEPA).[26] Persons targeted under these financial sanctions are said to be "designated" as either WMD proliferators or global terrorists, depending on which set of sanctions is employed, and any transactions with them by U.S. persons are prohibited.[27] According to Treasury, the goal of this action is to deny sanctioned parties' access to the U.S. financial and commercial systems. Treasury or State can make designations under these financial sanctions, which are published in the *Federal Register*.[28]

As of October 25, 2007, 53 of the 70 parties designated under the nonproliferation financial sanctions were tied to Iranian proliferation activities. Of these 53 parties, 48 were either Iranian entities or overseas subsidiaries of Iranian banks, 4 were Chinese, and 1 was American. Several designations have been made in recent months. For example, in June 2007, Treasury designated four Iranian companies for their role in Iran's proliferation of WMD.[29] On October 25, 2007, State and Treasury designated 27 entities or individuals under Executive Order 13382, including the Islamic Revolutionary Guard Corps (IRGC) [30] and other companies or individuals affiliated with the IRGC, the Ministry of Defense and Armed Forces Logistics, and two Iranian banks, including Bank Melli—Iran's largest bank.

With regard to the antiterrorism financial sanctions, Treasury was unable to provide us with data on the number of Iran-related designations because it does not compile information about the country or countries with which the designated entities are involved. We were, however, able to identify instances where antiterrorism financial sanctions were imposed. For example, on October 25, 2007, under Executive Order 13224, Treasury designated the IRGC's Qods Force a supporter of terrorism. According to Treasury, the Qods Force provides material support to the Taliban, Lebanese Hizbollah, Hamas, and other terrorist groups. Treasury also designated Iran's Bank Saderat, which is already subject to financial restrictions under the trade ban, as a terrorism financier.

Chapter 2

U.S. AGENCIES HAVE NOT ASSESSED THE OVERALL IMPACT OF SANCTIONS TARGETING IRAN

U.S. officials and experts report that U.S. sanctions are having specific impacts on Iran; however, the extent of such impacts is difficult to determine, and agencies have not assessed the overall impact of sanctions. First, U.S. officials report that U.S. sanctions have slowed foreign investment in Iran's petroleum sector, which hinders Iran's ability to fund proliferation and terrorism-related activities. Second, financial sanctions deny parties involved in Iran's proliferation and terrorism activities access to the U.S. financial system and complicate their support for such activities. Third, U.S. officials have identified broad impacts of sanctions, such as providing a clear statement of U.S. concerns about Iran. However, other evidence raises questions about the extent of reported economic impacts. Since 2003, the Iranian government has signed contracts reported at approximately $20 billion with foreign firms to develop its energy resources, though it is uncertain whether these contracts will ultimately be carried out. In addition, sanctioned Iranian banks may be able to turn to other financial sources or fund their activities in currencies other than the U.S. dollar. U.S. and international reports also find that Iran continues proliferation activities and support for terrorism. Finally, U.S. agencies, except for Treasury's assessments of its financial sanctions under Executive Orders 13382 and 13224, do not assess the impact of sanctions in helping achieve U.S. objectives nor collect data demonstrating the direct results of their sanctioning and enforcement actions.

Agencies Report that Sanctions Have Delayed Investment in Iran's Petroleum Sector and Had Other Impacts

State and Treasury officials report that sanctions have had specific impacts such as delaying foreign investment in Iran's petroleum sector and reducing Iran's access to the U.S. financial system. In addition, broad impacts of sanctions, such as their symbolic value, also have been recognized.

U.S. Officials State that Iran Sanctions Act Has Contributed to Delays in Foreign Investment in Iran's Petroleum Sector

U.S. officials and experts have stated that U.S. sanctions have played a role in slowing Iran's progress in developing its oil and gas resources. The Iran Sanctions Act is intended to limit investment in Iran's petroleum sector, with an expectation that curbing such investment would disrupt the revenue generated by new oil and gas investments and reduce Iran's ability to pursue policies that the United States deemed unacceptable. A 2004 State Department report noted that the law had, among other things, helped delay investment in Iran's petroleum sector.[31] According to State Department officials, there have been no new final oil and gas investment deals in Iran since 2004. Other experts have similarly noted a slowdown in investment in Iran's oil and gas sectors and have cited statements that Iranian oil officials had made to that effect. U.S. officials and experts have also noted that, while the existence of the Iran Sanctions Act and its use as a tool for dialogue with foreign parties may be a contributing factor to a slowdown in foreign investment in Iran, Iran's own investment policies[32] may be contributing to a reduced flow of investment.

On the other hand, the Department of State has raised concerns about possible energy deals between Iran and potential foreign investors, including the reported $16 billion China National Offshore Oil Corporation deal for the development of Iran's North Pars gas field. Further, the United States has expressed concerns about the estimated $4.3 billion preliminary agreement that Royal Dutch Shell, along with Spain's Repsol, concluded with the Iranian regime for the construction of a liquefied natural gas plant at South Pars, the world's largest natural gas field. Also, Indian firms have entered into contracts in recent years for the purchase of Iranian gas and oil. The proposed construction of a pipeline to deliver Iranian natural gas to India through Pakistan is a project about which the United States has expressed concerns.

We also found that since 2003 the Iranian government has signed contracts reported at approximately $20 billion with foreign firms to develop Iran's energy resources. It is uncertain whether these contracts will ultimately be carried out, and at least one has already been withdrawn. However, these agreements demonstrate foreign firms' significant interest in financing or underwriting projects in Iran's energy sector. (See app. IV for a listing of recent major agreements between Iran and foreign investors in Iran's energy sector.)[33]

U.S. Officials Report that Financial Sanctions Deny Entities Involved in Proliferation and Terrorism Access to U.S. Financial System

State and Treasury officials have testified that financial sanctions deny designated individuals and entities access to the funds needed to sustain Iran's proliferation.[34] For example, in January 2007, the U.S. government designated Bank Sepah under Executive Order 13382 as a supporter of WMD proliferation, thereby eliminating its access to the U.S. financial system and reducing its ability to conduct dollar transactions.[35] Further, U.S. financial sanctions also have reportedly disrupted Iran's support for terrorism. U.S. officials report that the United States has disrupted Hizbollah's financial support network by reducing the ability of Iranian banks to interact with the U.S. financial system. For example, in September 2006, Treasury altered the trade ban regulations to cut off Bank Saderat, Iran's second largest state-owned bank, from dollar transactions due to its support for terrorism.[36] Treasury officials reported that Iran used Bank Saderat to move millions of dollars to terrorist organizations such as Hizbollah, Hamas, and the Palestinian Islamic Jihad. This action complicated the bank's financial transactions and alerted the world's financial community to Bank Saderat's role in funding terrorism.

However, Iran may be able to find alternative financial sources or fund its activities in currencies other than the dollar. Treasury officials have noted that sanctioned parties often find "workarounds" to lessen the sanctions impact, and other financial options can be used.[37] For example, sanctioned Iranian banks may turn to euro or other currency transactions to support

Iranian government activities. Further, in 2006, a Treasury official testified that stopping money flows to Iran is particularly challenging because the Iranian government draws upon a large network of state-owned banks and parastatal companies that is difficult to penetrate.

State and Treasury officials further reported that the effects of U.S. financial sanctions have been augmented because several large European banks, responding to U.S. diplomatic efforts, have curtailed their business with sanctioned Iranian entities and are refraining from conducting dollar transactions with Iran. At least 7 of the banks that have limited or ended their dealings with sanctioned Iranian entities rank among the 20 largest European banks.[38] U.S officials also report that a number of governments, including France, Germany, Italy, and Japan, are beginning to reduce their export credits[39] for goods shipped to Iran.[40] U.S. officials have contended that such developments have made it increasingly difficult for Iran to execute important financial transactions necessary for Iran's domestic energy and other projects. U.S. agency officials and experts also have cited the increased costs[41] to Iran of obtaining finance and goods, sometimes resulting in inferior component parts. State officials assert that as more countries limit their financial interactions with Iranian entities and individuals engaging in suspect activities, these parties have been denied access to major financial and commercial systems.

Experts and Officials Recognize that Sanctions Have Other Broad Impacts

U.S. officials and sanction experts state that sanctions have other broad impacts. For example, State officials stressed that U.S. sanctions serve as a clear symbolic statement to the rest of the world of U.S. concerns regarding Iran's proliferation and terrorism-related activities. State officials also noted that sanction laws can be used as a vehicle for dialogue with foreign companies or countries, and the prospect of sanctions can encourage foreign parties to end their interactions with Iran. Finally, U.S. officials have stated that publicly identifying entities and listing them in the *Federal Register* may deter other firms from engaging in business with sanctioned entities.[42]

IRAN HALTED ITS NUCLEAR WEAPONS PROGRAM BUT CONTINUES TO ENRICH URANIUM, ACQUIRE ADVANCED WEAPONS, AND SUPPORT TERRORISM

The extent of the sanctions' impact in deterring Iran from proliferation activities, acquiring advanced weapons technology, and support for terrorism is unclear. Although Iran halted its nuclear weapons program, it continues to enrich uranium, acquire advanced weapons, and support terrorism. According to the November 2007 U.S. National Intelligence Estimate, Iran halted its nuclear weapons program in the fall of 2003. According to the estimate, Iranian military entities were working under government direction to develop nuclear weapons. However, Iran halted the program because of international scrutiny and pressure resulting from exposure of Iran's previously undeclared nuclear activities. (See app. II for a timeline of UN and international actions with regard to Iran's enrichment activities.)

Although it has halted its nuclear weapons program, Iran continues its uranium enrichment program. While enriched uranium can be used for nuclear weapons, Iran has stated that its program is for peaceful civilian purposes. The Director General of the International Atomic Energy Agency[43] (IAEA) stated on September 17, 2007, that Iran had not suspended its enrichment activities and continued to build its heavy water reactor at Arak. This announcement followed a series of IAEA discoveries about Iran's nuclear program. In 2002, the IAEA was informed of a previously undeclared nuclear enrichment plant in Natanz and a heavy water plant in Arak.[44] Subsequent IAEA inspections revealed that Iran had made significant progress toward mastering the technology to make enriched uranium.

Iran also continues to acquire advanced weapons technology, including ballistic missile technology, according to Treasury. According to State officials, Chinese entities supply certain dual-use items to Iran, including some that U.S. officials believe could be used in support of Iran's WMD, ballistic and cruise missiles, or advanced conventional weapons programs.

The U.S. government also reports that Iran continues to support terrorism. We have reported that Iran is one of several countries from which Islamic extremism is currently being propagated.[45] In addition, according to State's 2006 *Country Report on Terrorism*, Iran continues to be an active state sponsor of terrorism.[46] The report states that the IRGC and Ministry of Intelligence and Security influence Palestinian groups in Syria and the Lebanese Hizbollah to use terrorism in pursuit of their goals. The report also noted that Iran provided guidance and training to select Iraqi Shi'a political groups and weapons and training to Shi'a militant groups to enable anticoalition attacks. In July 2007, officials of U.S. intelligence agencies testified that Iran regards its ability to conduct terrorism operations as a key element of its national security strategy.

U.S. Agencies Do Not Assess the Overall Impact of Sanctions and Lack Data on Sanction Results

U.S. agencies do not assess the overall impact of sanctions in deterring Iran's proliferation, acquisition of advanced weapons technology, or terrorism-related activities, noting the difficulty of isolating the impact of sanctions from all other factors that influence Iran's behavior. In addition, except for Treasury assessments of financial sanctions, agencies do not possess data on the direct results of sanctions, such as the types of goods seized that violate the trade ban or the subsequent behavior of parties that sell prohibited goods to Iran.

Agency Officials Cite Difficulties Measuring the Overall Impact of Sanctions on Iran

State, Treasury, and Commerce officials said that they do not measure the overall impact of sanctions they implement. For example, both State and Treasury officials emphasized that, with one exception regarding one sanction law, they have not attempted to measure the ability of U.S. sanctions to deter Iran's proliferation or terrorism-related activities. State officials stated it is not possible to isolate the impact of sanctions from all other factors that influence Iran's behavior, such as the actions of other countries. Further, State officials reported that sanctions are just one component of U.S. efforts to influence Iran's behavior.

Treasury officials conduct classified assessments of entities designated under Executive Orders 13382 and 13224, but report that they do not assess the overall impact of sanctions, stating it can be difficult to differentiate the impact of various U.S. efforts. For example, it is difficult to know where the effects of U.S. diplomacy end and the effects of U.S. sanctions begin. State and Treasury officials noted that, while the goal of sanctions is to change

Iran's behavior, such changes take time, and it is not possible to track how sanctions imposed today might affect overall behavior in the future. Such an exercise would be extremely difficult due to the challenges associated with establishing any causal linkage between U.S. sanctions and Iran's subsequent behavior. In addition, agency officials noted that the sanctions targeting Iran do not constitute a separate program or line of effort; thus, these activities are not monitored or assessed separately. However, according to Treasury officials, sanctions implemented by OFAC constitute a separate program with its own set of regulations (the Iranian Transaction Regulations) and OFAC does focus specific effort on Iran sanctions. Finally, Treasury and Commerce officials stated that it would be difficult to measure either the deterrent impact of sanctions or, conversely, the extent to which illegal or sanctionable activities continue undetected.

In 2004, State completed a review of the Iran Sanctions Act (then known as the Iran-Libya Sanctions Act). The ILSA Extension Act of 2001 required the President to provide Congress with a report describing the extent to which the act had been effective in denying Iran the ability to support acts of international terrorism and fund the acquisition of WMD by limiting Iran's ability to develop its petroleum resources.[47] This report stated that actions taken pursuant to the act had a "modest positive impact." The 2004 report is the only formal assessment U.S. agencies have completed on the broad impact of sanctions against Iran.

Agencies Lack Data on Direct Sanction Results

In addition, agency officials do not possess data on the direct results of sanctions. For example, regarding the trade ban, officials from DHS's Customs and Border Protection reported that inspectors are not required to document whether or not a given seizure is related to the ban. As a result, they are unable to provide complete data on the volume or nature of goods seized that violate this ban. Further, although Treasury posts on the Internet its OFAC administrative penalties, it does not compile information regarding the number of cases that involve violations of Iran sanctions (we were able to identify such cases after reviewing more than 400 detailed case descriptions) and the nature of such violations. FBI officials said that, within their counterintelligence division, they classify investigations by country of origin but would not be able to distinguish cases involving Iran sanctions from other Iran-related cases because the bureau's automated data systems do not include such information. In addition, complete DHS/ICE data on

Iran sanctions cases are not available because ICE agents are not required to document the country of destination when opening a case, nor is this information always subsequently added as the case progresses. Further, a Justice official stated that the department prosecutes and organizes its cases by statute and does not classify its cases by the specific country or nationality of the individual involved in its data system. It is thus not possible to identify cases specific to the trade and investment ban with Iran. In addition, although agencies cite transshipment as a key means of evading the trade ban, they do not collect data that would help illustrate the magnitude of the problem.

Further, State does not review whether sanctions imposed under the law currently known as the Iran, North Korea, and Syria Nonproliferation Act—the law used most frequently to sanction foreign parties—stop sanctioned parties from engaging in proliferation activities with Iran or are relevant for these parties. The law does not require such a review. State officials said that, while they are aware of instances where proliferation activities ended following the imposition of sanctions on particular firms, such information is primarily collected on an anecdotal basis. There has been no overall or systematic review of whether sanctioned entities ended their proliferation activities, though State officials indicated that they monitor the activities of sanctioned parties as part of their daily responsibilities. Further, these officials emphasized that State must apply the sanctions established by law, such as a prohibition on participating in U.S. government procurement opportunities, regardless of their relevance or potential impact. State officials acknowledged the likelihood that the sanctions established by law may have limited relevance for sanctioned parties, which may be illustrated in cases where the same parties are sanctioned repeatedly for proliferation activities with Iran.

In addition, OFAC does not compile data on the value of assets frozen pursuant to targeted financial sanctions. OFAC tracks information on assets frozen in the aggregate, not by the amount of assets frozen for each particular party that is sanctioned. OFAC also did not have information regarding the number of parties sanctioned under Iran-related antiterrorism financial sanctions. According to OFAC, systematically tracking these data and information is not a useful measure of the efficacy of sanctions.

Chapter 3

IRAN'S GLOBAL TRADE TIES LIMIT U.S. SANCTION INFLUENCE ON IRAN'S BEHAVIOR; UN SANCTIONS HAVE RECENTLY BEEN IMPOSED

Iran's global trade ties and leading role in energy production make it difficult for the United States to isolate Iran and deter its acquisition of advanced weapons technology and support for terrorism. First, Iran's trade with the world—both imports and exports—has grown since the U.S. trade ban began in 1987. Although trade has fluctuated from year to year, most of the growth has occurred since 2002, coinciding with the rise in oil prices. This trade includes imports of weapons and nuclear technology. Second, global interest in purchasing and developing Iran's substantial petroleum reserves has kept Iran active in global commerce. Iran's integration in the world economy has complicated U.S. efforts to encourage other countries to isolate Iran; however, multilateral efforts targeting Iran have recently begun. Beginning in December 2006, the UNSC adopted sanctions against Iran in response to Iran's noncompliance with its international obligations. These sanctions are still being implemented.

IRAN'S STRONG GLOBAL TRADE MAKES IT DIFFICULT FOR U.S. SANCTIONS TO PRESSURE IRAN

Over the past 20 years, U.S. trade with Iran has decreased, but Iran's trade with the rest of the world has increased, in large part due to increases in oil prices between 2002 and 2006. Asian countries, particularly China, are increasing their trade with Iran. Countries such as China and Russia continue to provide Iran with sensitive goods.

Iran's Trade with the United States Decreased Substantially Following the Imposition of the Trade Ban

U.S. trade with Iran declined sharply immediately following the adoption of both the 1987 U.S. ban on imports from Iran and the 1995 ban on U.S. exports to and investment in Iran. However, U.S exports to Iran rebounded to some degree when the sanctions were eased in 2000. Before the 1987 U.S. import ban, 16 percent of Iran's total exports, primarily oil, were shipped to the United States. Following the ban, this share dropped to about .1 percent. According to our analysis of U.S. trade data, Iran exported $2 billion in goods to the United States in 1987, about $10 million in 1988, and less than $1 million annually for most of the 1990s.[48] Further, 2 percent of Iran's imports were from the United States before the export ban in 1995; this dropped to almost zero after the ban. Total U.S. exports to Iran declined from about $282 million in 1995 to less than $400,000 in 1996. By 2000, however, total U.S.-Iran trade had increased to about $218 million, largely as a result of the relaxation of the sanctions in that year to allow for the purchase and import of Iranian carpets. In 2006, total U.S.-Iran trade was $247 million.

Our analysis of U.S. trade data indicates that both the export and import declines coincided with significant changes in the types of goods traded. For example, the top U.S. exports to Iran prior to the 1995 export ban were in the UN trade category "nuclear reactors, boilers, and machinery," while the top exports immediately following the ban were in the category "printed books and other informational materials." In 2006, the top U.S. exports to Iran were pharmaceuticals and tobacco products. The top U.S. import from Iran before the 1987 import ban was oil, whereas the top import immediately following the ban—and also in 2006—was carpets and other textile floor coverings.

Iran's Overall Trade Has Grown Since 1987, and Its Trading Partners Are Diverse

Despite the ban of Iranian imports to the United States in 1987 and the ban on U.S. exports to Iran in 1995, Iran's overall trade has grown.[49] From 1987 through 2006, Iran's exports grew from $8.5 billion to $70 billion, while Iran's imports grew from $7 billion to $46 billion (see figure 2).[50] The annual real growth in Iran's exports between 1987 and 2006 was nearly 9 percent; however, the export growth rate between 2002 and 2006 was 19 percent, reflecting the steep rise in oil prices since 2002 (see figure 2).[51] Iran's imports grew at an average annual rate of about 7 percent between 1987 and 2006. Iran's exports and imports both fluctuated during this period. For example, Iran's imports increased significantly following the end of the Iran-Iraq war in 1988, followed by steep declines from 1993 to 1994, following Iran's major currency devaluation (over 1,800 percent). Likewise, Iran's exports fluctuated. The growth in Iran's exports from 1989 to 1993 was followed by a general decline through 1998. Exports grew dramatically from 2002 to 2006, coinciding with the rise in the price of oil from $25 to $65 a barrel. The overall growth in Iran's trade from 1986 to 2006 demonstrates the limits of the U.S. trade ban to isolate Iran and pressure it to reduce its proliferation activities and support for terrorism.

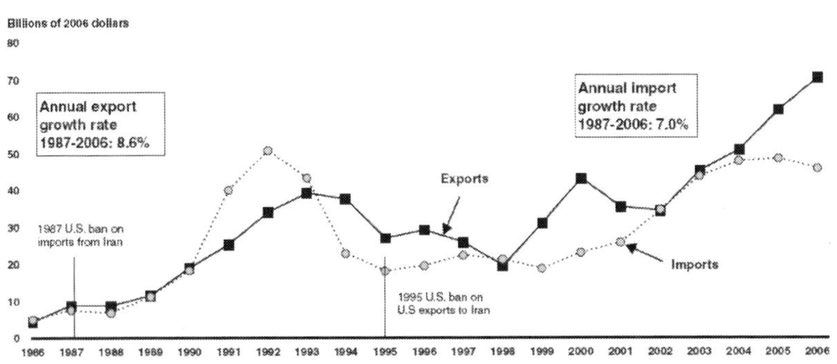

Source: GAO analysis of IMF Direction of Trade Statistics, May 2007.

Note: Iran's trade figures are provided in constant 2006 dollars using an alternative exchange rate developed by the World Bank (see app. I).

Figure 2. Iran's Total Exports and Imports, 1986-2006.

Figure 2 shows that in the year following the 1987 U.S. ban on Iranian imports, Iran's exports to the world did not decline. In fact, Iran's exports began growing dramatically in 1989. In the 2 years following the 1995 ban on U.S. exports to Iran, Iran's imports from the world grew, and have generally continued to grow. Iran has been able to readily replace the loss in U.S. trade through trade with other countries, and the total value of Iranian imports and exports has continued to grow largely uninterrupted.

In addition to the overall growth of Iran's trade since 1987, Iran has extensive global trade ties with Europe and the developing world. In particular, trade with Asian countries has nearly doubled since 1994.[52] Asian countries accounted for 30 percent of Iran's exports in 2006, up from about 16 percent in 1994. Iran's exports to China increased from about 1 percent in 1994 to about 13 percent in 2006. Japan and China were the top two recipients of exports from Iran, together accounting for more than one-quarter of Iran's exports in 2006 (see table 2).

Table 2. Iran's Top Export Market s, by Country, 1994 and 2006

Millions of 2006 dollars					
Country	1994		2006		
	Dollar amount	Share of Iran's total exports	Country	Dollar amount	Share of Iran's total exports
Japan	$5,632	15.1%	Japan	$9,941	14.2%
United States	5,184	13.9	China	9,194	13.1
United Kingdom	3,427	9.2	Turkey	5,112	7.3
Germany	2,303	6.2	Italy	4,451	6.3
Korea	1,776	4.8	Korea	4,040	5.8
Turkey	1,656	4.4	Netherlands	3,263	4.6
UAE	1,493	4.0	South Africa	2,710	3.9
Italy	1,452	3.9	France	2,710	3.9
Greece	1,349	3.6	Spain	2,275	3.2
Singapore	1,344	3.6	Greece	2,066	2.9
All other	11,600	31.2	All other	24,420	34.8
Total	$37,217	100.0	Total	$70,181	100.0

Source: GAO analysis of IMF Direction of Trade Statistics, May 2007.
Note: Percentages may not add to 100 due to rounding.

Iran's growing trade with China has played a large role in replacing the declining share of EU countries' trade with Iran over the past decade and contributing to Iran's growing trade with Asian countries. In 2006, the EU accounted for nearly one-quarter of Iran's exports to the world, down from 33 percent in 1994. Germany and the United Kingdom were part of this decline. From 1994 to 2006, Iran's exports to Germany declined from about

6 percent to less than 1 percent and from about 9 percent to less than 1 percent for the United Kingdom.

In 2006, Germany and China were Iran's largest providers of imports, accounting for 23 percent of Iran's imports. Although Germany has remained the largest supplier of imports to Iran for over a decade, its share of Iran's imports has declined from about 19 percent in 1994 to 12 percent in 2006, while Iran's imports from China increased from about 1 percent in 1994 to about 11 percent in 2006 (see table 3). Iran increased its imports from Middle East countries from about 8 percent to 13 percent, with UAE's share increasing from over 5 percent in 1994 to about 9 percent in 2006.

Table 3. Iran's Top Import Suppliers, by Country, 1994 and 2006

Millions of 2006 dollars					
Country	1994	2006			
	Dollar amount	Share of Iran's total imports	Country	Dollar amount	Share of Iran's total imports
Germany	$4,231	18.7%	Germany	$5,631	12.3%
Italy	1,931	8.5	China	5,020	11.0
Japan	1,712	7.6	UAE	3,972	8.7
Belguim-Luxembourg	1,246	5.5	Korea	2,908	6.4
UAE	1,239	5.5	France	2,615	5.7
United Kingdom	1,041	4.6	Italy	2,537	5.6
France	917	4.1	Russia	1,680	3.7
Azerbaijan	751	3.3	India	1,616	3.5
United States	665	2.9	Brazil	1,315	2.9
Korea	612	2.7	Japan	1,287	2.8
All other	8,243	36.5	All other	17,041	37.4
Total	$22,588	100.0	Total	$45,624	100.0

Source: GAO analysis of IMF Direction of Trade Statistics, May 2007.
Note: Percentages may not add to 100 due to rounding.

A regional shift in Iran's import suppliers also took place between 1994 and 2006. The EU's share of Iran's imports from the world declined from 50.5 percent in 1994 to slightly over one-third of Iran's imports in 2006, while Asian countries' share has tripled, from 9 percent to 27 percent.

Other Countries Continue to Provide Weapons and Nuclear Technology to Iran

Other countries' exports to Iran include dual-use or sensitive goods, such as arms, aircraft, and nuclear equipment and technology–goods that the U.S. statutorily prohibits from export to Iran. For example, according to UN trade data, Russia and Spain exported $28.9 million of nuclear reactor parts from 2004 to 2005, over 89 percent from Russia. Iran also acquired spare parts to U.S.-made fighter jets, parts that were sold to other countries as surplus.[53] According to State officials, Chinese entities supply certain dual-use items to Iran, including some that U.S. officials believe could be used in support of Iran's WMD, ballistic missile, cruise missiles, or advanced conventional weapons programs. According to a CRS report[54] and the testimony from U.S. intelligence agencies, Iran is becoming self-sufficient in the production of ballistic missiles, largely with foreign help. Iran is also an important customer for Russia's weapons and civil nuclear technology. Additional information detailing Iran's purchases of weapons and nuclear technology is classified.

Iran's Prominent Oil-Producing and Exporting Role Limits the Impact of Sanctions

Demand for Iranian crude oil, coupled with high oil prices, helps support Iran's economy and limits the effects of the U.S. trade ban. Iran is a prominent world oil producer, and its economy relies heavily on oil export revenues. Iran ranked fourth in terms of world oil production and exports in 2005, exporting about 2.6 million barrels of oil per day. Iran has the third largest proven oil reserves and the second largest reserves of natural gas worldwide,[55] according to the Oil and Gas Journal. Oil export revenues represent nearly 80 percent of Iran's total merchandise export earnings and accounted for about 19 percent of Iran's GDP in 2004.

In 2005, Japan and China accounted for 27 and 14 percent of Iran's crude oil exports, respectively, as shown in table 4. [56]

Given the strong demand for Iranian crude oil, bolstered by continuing support for Iran's non-oil exports, several private sector and U.S. economic experts stated that Iran's near-term growth prospects look favorable. However, a sharp drop in oil prices is a risk, and, according to the IMF, a further escalation of tensions associated with nuclear issues would adversely affect investment and growth.[57] Another concern is Iran's growing gasoline consumption, which is heavily subsidized by the government. According to the Department of Energy, Iran is the second largest importer of gasoline in the world after the United States and has a shortage of refining capacity to produce gasoline.[58] In 2006, as part of the Iranian government's effort to reduce the subsidy on gasoline, the government raised the price of gasoline 25 percent and introduced "smart cards" in an effort to deter gas smuggling, reduce gasoline shortages, and improve the budget situation.[59] In addition, according to economic experts, Iran has benefited from strong growth in non-oil exports in recent years.[60] Non-oil exports increase the resiliency of Iran's economy and mitigate its vulnerability to falling oil prices, as well as provide jobs. As part of the government's policy to move away from crude oil exports, Iran is expanding its petrochemical production capacity and moving toward export of petrochemical products.[61]

Table 4. Top Iranian Crude Oil Export Destinations and Country Share, 2005

Country	Share of Iran's crude oil exports
Japan	27.3%
China	14.4
Italy	9.0
South Korea	8.9
France	7.0
Turkey	6.5
South Africa	6.1
Greece	5.0
Spain	4.7
Philippines	2.8
All other countries	8.2
Total	100.0

Source: GAO analysis of UN Trade Statistics, Iran's exports of oil (commodity grouping, HS2709), other countries reporting, 1989-2005.
Note: Percentages may not add to 100 due to rounding.

UN Established Multilateral Sanctions against Iran in 2006

Multilateral efforts targeting Iran resulted in the imposition of UN sanctions in 2006 as a result of concerns that Iran's nuclear program might contain a weapons-related component. In July 2006, UNSC resolution 1696 demanded that Iran suspend its uranium enrichment program by August 2006 or face possible sanctions.[62] Iran did not suspend these activities, and in December 2006, the UNSC unanimously approved UNSC resolution 1737.[63] This resolution prohibits UN member states from supplying Iran with the nuclear and missile-related materials or technology specified in the resolution, as well as any other items that would contribute to proliferation-sensitive nuclear activities or the development of nuclear weapon delivery systems. In addition, UN member states are required to freeze the financial assets and other economic resources of individuals and entities designated by the UNSC as having ties to Iran's nuclear or ballistic missile programs. Further, the resolution provides for a ban on the provision of financial services related to the supply, sale, manufacture, transfer or use of prohibited items specified in the resolution. Iran was required to suspend its enrichment-related, reprocessing, and heavy water-related activities and cooperate fully with the IAEA by February 2007 or face possible additional sanctions.

The UNSC imposed further sanctions on Iran after the IAEA found that it did not suspend its enrichment or heavy water-related activities. In March 2007, the UNSC passed resolution 1747,[64] which banned arms exports from Iran; called upon all UN member states to exercise restraint in sales to Iran of certain categories of heavy conventional arms; designated additional individuals and entities, including Bank Sepah and those affiliated with the IRGC, as subject to the asset freeze requirement; and urged UN member states and international financial institutions not to enter into new commitments for financial assistance to the government of Iran, except for humanitarian and developmental purposes. Resolution 1747 reaffirmed Iran's obligation to suspend its enrichment, reprocessing, and heavy water-related activities and affirmed UNSC intentions to consider additional sanctions should Iran fail to comply by May 2007. The IAEA Director General confirmed Iran's failure to comply in its report of May 2007. State officials noted that this report triggered ongoing consultations among six countries regarding next steps, including the possible adoption of additional sanctions. [65]

UNSC resolution 1737 established a sanctions committee charged with monitoring implementation by UN member states of the measures imposed under the resolution, including by reviewing required country compliance reports. The State Department reported that, as of August 2007, the UNSC 1737 Sanctions Committee had received reports from 82 UN member countries (43 percent) on resolution 1737 and reports from 64 UN member countries (33 percent) on resolution 1747.

U.S. officials have stated that UN sanctions enhance the international credibility of U.S. sanctions and provide leverage to increase pressure on Iran. State officials have noted that multilateral sanctions enhance the potential effectiveness of U.S. sanctions. Since UN sanctions have been in place for about a year, it is difficult to assess their impact.

Chapter 4

CONCLUSION

For the past 20 years, U.S. sanctions against Iran have been an important element of U.S. policy to deter Iran from weapons proliferation and support for terrorism. Congress is considering additional sanctions targeting Iran. UN sanctions may also play an important role in pressuring Iran, but these sanctions have not yet been fully implemented. However, the overall impact of sanctions, and the extent to which these sanctions further U.S. objectives, is unclear. On the other hand, some evidence, such as foreign firms signing contracts to invest in Iran's energy sector and Iran's continued proliferation efforts, raise questions about the extent of the sanctions' impact. Moreover, U.S. agencies do not systematically collect information on the direct results of the multiple sanctions they implement, or their data do not provide specific information on Iran sanctions. These agencies have not conducted a baseline assessment of the impact of the sanctions. Collecting data on the results of multiple sanctions against Iran and conducting an overall baseline assessment is challenging, given all the agencies involved and the complexities of collecting some of the necessary information. However, without an overall assessment of the sanctions' impact and subsequent reviews on a periodic basis, the Congress and the Administration will continue to lack important information for developing effective strategies to influence Iran's behavior.

Chapter 5

MATTER FOR CONGRESSIONAL CONSIDERATION

Congress and the Administration need a better understanding of the impact of U.S. sanctions against Iran and the extent to which sanctions are achieving U.S. foreign policy objectives. The Administration needs to take a series of actions to first improve the disparate data collected on Iran sanctions and then establish baseline information for the continuous monitoring and periodic reporting on what U.S. sanctions have achieved. Accordingly, we recommend that Congress consider requiring the NSC, in collaboration with the Departments of State, the Treasury, Energy, and Commerce; the intelligence community; and U.S. enforcement agencies to take the following actions:

(1) collect, analyze, and improve data on U.S. agencies' actions to enforce sanctions against Iran and complete an overall baseline assessment of the impact and use of U.S. sanctions, including factors that impair or strengthen them. This assessment should collect information, to the extent feasible, from various U.S. agencies and consider factors such as, but not limited to, the following:

- the number of goods seized, penalties imposed, and convictions obtained under the trade ban (Homeland Security, Treasury, Commerce, Justice);
- sensitive items diverted to Iran through transshipment points (Commerce and the intelligence community);
- the extent to which repeat foreign violators of Iran-specific sanctions laws have ended their sales of sensitive items to Iran (State and intelligence community);

- the amount of assets frozen resulting from financial sanctions (Treasury and the intelligence community); and
- the extent of delays in foreign investment in Iran's energy sector (State, Energy, and the intelligence community).

(2) develop a framework for assessing the ongoing impact of U.S. sanctions, taking into account any data gaps that were identified as part of the baseline assessment , and the contribution of multilateral sanctions.

(3) report periodically to the Congress on the impact of sanctions against Iran in achieving U.S. foreign policy objectives.

Chapter 6

AGENCY COMMENTS AND EVALUATION

We provided a draft of this report to the Departments of State, the Treasury, Commerce, Defense, Energy, Justice, and Homeland Security. We also provided a draft to the NSC and the Office of the Director of National Intelligence (ODNI). The Department of the Treasury provided a formal response emphasizing that, as a result of financial pressure, Iran is experiencing increasing isolation from the global community. The department's response also states that Iran continues to pursue nuclear capabilities and ballistic missile technology and to fund terrorism. This comment reinforces our finding that the overall impact of sanctions is unclear. In addition, the Treasury noted its assessments of the effectiveness of financial sanctions. We revised the report to recognize that Treasury assesses the impact of financial sanctions but maintain that an overall impact assessment of all U.S. sanctions has not been undertaken. Finally, Treasury commented that the amount of assets blocked under available financial sanctions is not a measure of the program's value. The department also noted that other sanction effects, such as the inability of designated parties to use the U.S. financial system or the reputational harm that stems from a designation, can often be the primary way sanctions have an international impact. We have noted the broad positive benefits of sanctions in our report. Treasury also told us in an earlier communication that it did not disagree with the part of our Matter for Congressional Consideration calling for an assessment of assets frozen using these financial tools. Treasury's letter can be found in appendix V.

The Departments of State, the Treasury, Commerce, and Energy provided written technical comments. We incorporated these comments into the report as appropriate. The Department of Commerce submitted its technical comments in a letter that is included in appendix VI. The NSC provided brief oral comments and ODNI provided a classified response; we considered this information and revised the report as appropriate. The Departments of Defense, Justice, and Homeland Security provided no comments on the draft report, though Homeland Security supported the part of our Matter for Congressional Consideration that specifically involves the department.

Chapter 7

APPENDIX I: OBJECTIVES, SCOPE, AND METHODOLOGY

The Ranking Member of the House Subcommittee on National Security and Foreign Affairs of the Committee on Oversight and Governmental Reform requested that we review U.S. sanctions involving Iran. This report addresses (1) U.S. sanctions targeting Iran and their implementation, (2) the reported impact of the sanctions, and (3) factors that limit the ability of U.S. sanctions to reduce Iran's proliferation and terrorism-related activities.

To identify U.S. sanctions targeting Iran and determine the U.S. efforts to implement and assess sanctions against Iran, we first identified, reviewed, and summarized U.S. executive orders and laws that establish sanctions and are targeted at Iran. While we focused on Iran-specific sanctions, we also reviewed targeted financial sanctions that address proliferation and terrorism concerns and can be used against any party, including Iran. In addition, we discussed the sanctions with officials from the Departments of State, Treasury, Commerce, Defense, Energy, Homeland Security (DHS), and Justice, as well as the Central Intelligence Agency.

We submitted several requests for specific data to help illustrate U.S. trade ban implementation and enforcement efforts; however, in many cases agencies were not able to fully answer our requests. Due to limitations in how agencies collect and organize their information, we were unable to collect complete data on export licenses issued by Treasury, or Customs and Border Protection seizures, Federal Bureau of Investigation (FBI) or Immigration and Customs Enforcement investigations, or Justice criminal convictions related to sanctions against Iran. We could not compile comprehensive data on the number of ongoing FBI investigations because the FBI considers such data sensitive. We were able to collect data on the extent of civil penalties imposed by Treasury, which we assessed to be sufficiently reliable for our purposes of showing the number of Iran-specific sanction violations since 2003. We were also able to collect data on the number of post-shipment verification checks conducted by Commerce in the past 5 years, which GAO has previously assessed as reliable.

To determine the use of Iran-specific laws to impose sanctions, we reviewed and compiled publicly available information on the Department of State's Web site (www.state.gov/t/isn/c15231.htm), reviewed relevant *Federal Register* notices, and additional information that was declassified. We determined that such data are sufficiently reliable for our purposes. State officials explained that they do not collect data on direct sanction results, emphasizing that such data falls within the purview of the intelligence community. Regarding the targeted financial sanctions, we were able to collect data on Iran-related designations made under the nonproliferation sanctions, which we determined to be sufficiently reliable. However, Treasury could not provide data on designations made under the antiterrorism sanctions or specify the amount of assets frozen under either set of financial sanctions.

To obtain U.S. government views on the impact of sanctions on Iran, we collected publicly available testimonies, speeches, and other remarks made by U.S. officials from the Departments of State, Commerce, Treasury, and DHS from March 2006 through April 2007. We reviewed these documents for statements regarding the U.S. government's position on the impacts of sanctions on Iran, factors that might lessen their impact, UN sanctions, and other issues identified as key to the U.S. foreign policy strategy for Iran. We also interviewed U.S. officials as well as a judgmentally selected group of experts from think tanks and universities and reviewed numerous scholarly articles and testimonies to gain additional perspectives on the impact of sanctions on Iran. After reviewing the literature on Iran sanctions and conducting a Web-based search of universities and other institutions with research projects or issue areas focusing on U.S. policies toward Iran, we identified a large field of experts. To balance our selection of experts to interview, we identified the institutions with which they were affiliated. These 39 institutions represented a wide variety of perspectives on U.S. foreign policy and, within them, we identified 56 scholars who have written papers and given presentations on Iran sanctions. We then selected six prominent scholars, each from an institution having a different political perspective, and with multiple publications on Iran sanctions. After reviewing their publications and speeches, we interviewed them on a set of questions concerning the impact of unilateral and UN sanctions against Iran, factors that might hinder impact, and other issues identified as key to U.S. foreign policy strategy for Iran.

To obtain information on the impact of sanctions in deterring investment in Iran's energy sector, FACTS Global Energy provided us with a list of recent major agreements between Iran and foreign firms and governments. FACTS Global Energy explained, in response to our questions concerning its methodology and the value of the contracts, that these are publicly reported figures, though the actual worth of the contract may be slightly higher or lower. While FACTS reports that some contracts are legally binding, Iran has been involved in several instances in which these contracts have not been fulfilled. We also substantiated many of these reported agreements based on our review of a variety of sources, including expert reports (Congressional Research Service [CRS], Economist Intelligence, Global Insight, Energy Information Administration); scholarly articles; testimony of senior U.S. officials; and other experts. Based on our interviews and checks, we determine the data were sufficiently reliable for the purposes of indicating the estimated value of publicly announced binding contracts between foreign companies and Iran.

To determine the major factors that affect U.S. sanctions ability to influence Iran's behavior, we reviewed numerous scholarly articles, professional economists' publications, official U.S. documents, and testimonies of officials and experts. In addition, we read open-source documents, including newspaper and journal articles, both national and global. We also interviewed a selected group of experts on Iran, met with agency officials, and attended conferences on the subject. In addition, we collected and analyzed data from several widely used databases of international trade statistics, including International Monetary Fund (IMF) Direction of Trade Statistics and International Financial Statistics National Income database, the UN trade database, U.S. Department of Commerce Trade Statistics, Department of Energy statistics, and United Nations Conference on Trade and Development Foreign Direct Investment statistics. We also reviewed and analyzed proprietary private sector data from an internationally recognized consultant on Iran's energy sector. We have determined that these data are sufficiently reliable for the purposes for which they were used in this report.

To determine the effect of U.S. sanctions on U.S. trade with Iran, we used 1986 to 2006 U.S. trade statistics from the Department of Commerce, Bureau of the Census Web-based database. We converted these data from nominal dollars to 2006 dollars using Department of Commerce, Bureau of Economic Analysis U.S. export and import commodity price deflators from the online database. We also analyzed these data at the 2-digit commodity level to determine what goods the United States exported to and imported from Iran in various years and the relative importance of U.S. trade to Iran for various years encompassing the imposition of the trade bans.

We used IMF Direction of Trade Statistics (May 2007 CD ROM) to analyze trends in Iran's trade, exports and imports, as well as Iran's trade with the world by major country groupings and individual partners, from 1986 to 2006.[1] We determined that the U.S. commodity price deflators noted above were not appropriate deflators for the purpose of analyzing Iran's global trade. Thus, we converted the annual export and import data, which IMF reports in U.S. dollars, into 2006 dollars using the following methodology. We converted annual dollar trade flows to Iranian rials using an exchange rate conversion factor from the *World Bank's World Development Indicators Online*. This conversion factor, known as the DEC alternative conversion factor, is, as a rule, the official exchange rate reported in the IMF's *International Financial Statistics*. This alternative conversion factor differs from the official rate when the official exchange rate is judged to diverge by an exceptionally large margin from the rate actually applied in international transactions.[2] In such cases, it employs a method known as the Atlas method to average exchange rates for a given year and the two preceding years, adjusted for differenced in rates of inflation between the country and a specified groups of major trading countries.[3] For 1991 and 1992, for which the World Bank does not publish a DEC alternative conversion factor for Iran, we constructed conversion rates by applying rates of change exhibited in a purchasing power parity conversion rate for Iran, from the *World Development Indicators Online*, from 1990 to1993.

As Iran does not publish separate price indices for exports and imports, in their place we use the Iranian gross domestic product (GDP) deflator from the World Bank's *World Development Indicators Online* to convert trade flows into 2006 rials. We then use the official 2006 exchange rate (which happens to be the same as the DEC conversion factor) to express these trade flows in constant 2006 dollars. This methodology preserves the real growth rates computed in real Iranian rials. Thus, it reflects how Iran may view its global trade when adjusted for exchange rate anomalies and price inflation.

We obtained general information on other countries' trade in sensitive goods (arms, aircraft, and nuclear equipment and technology) from publicly available official sources, including State Department reports and testimonies, Department of Justice data, the unclassified National Intelligence Estimate, and CRS reports and testimonies. To identify countries and the value of their exports to Iran of possibly sensitive items, we used the global shipping company DHL's online interactive product classification tool to identify Harmonized System (HS) trade codes in the export control category 0: Nuclear materials, facilities, equipment and miscellaneous items. We then used the UN trade database to identify countries and their reported value of exports to Iran for these items.

The Department of Energy's Energy Information Administration (EIA) provided data on Iran's position in world oil and gas reserves and production, gasoline consumption, and export earnings.[4] We calculated Iran's oil export revenue as a percent of Iran's GDP using reporting countries' crude oil import statistics from Iran[5] and GDP data from the most currently available IMF International Financial Statistics CD ROM (December 2006). To determine top Iranian crude oil export destinations and respective country shares, we used UN trade statistics at the 2-digit commodity level (HS2709), for the period 1989 to 2005, and ranked countries by dollar value and country share of crude oil exports from Iran. For the top recipients of Iran's crude oil, we also calculated each country's crude oil imports from Iran as a percent of that country's total crude oil imports to demonstrate the relative importance of Iranian crude oil to these countries. We also used 2-digit commodity level (HS2710 and HS2711) UN trade statistics to determine the major suppliers of refined petroleum products to Iran.

We based our assessment of Iran's near-term growth prospects on a review of economists' reports on Iran, including IMF's 2007 Article IV consultation with Iran and country reports on Iran from Economists Intelligence Unit and Global Insight. We also utilized proprietary information obtained from FACTS Global Energy regarding current developments in Iran's energy sector. We supplemented our review with reports on Iran from other official sources, including CRS and the Department of Energy's EIA.

To determine the development and current status of Iran's nuclear program, we reviewed documents from the International Atomic Energy Agency, an independent agency affiliated with the United Nations. We also reviewed reports by the CRS specific to Iran's nuclear program and proliferation concerns. Finally, we reviewed the November 2007 unclassified National Intelligence Estimate on Iran. We also reviewed State and other documents to examine Iran's broad proliferation efforts. To identify continued behavior by the government of Iran that establishes continued support for terrorism, we reviewed the Department of State's 2006 Country Report on Terrorism, other unclassified documentation (such as Department of State testimonies and CRS reports) as well as classified information.

To trace the development of UN sanctions against Iran for its efforts to enrich uranium and possibly develop nuclear weapon capability, we reviewed UN Security Council (UNSC) resolutions 1696 (2006), 1737 (2006), and 1747 (2007) and reports and documents from the UNSC 1737 Sanctions Committee. We also reviewed documentation from the Department of State and CRS. The State Department's Bureau for International Organization Affairs declined to meet with us, which precluded direct contact with the United Nations. The Bureau stated that negotiations in the UNSC were ongoing at the time.

We conducted our review from November 2006 to November 2007 in accordance with generally accepted government auditing standards.

Chapter 8

APPENDIX II: U.S. AND UN SANCTIONS TARGETING IRAN

U.S. government sanctions		International Atomic Energy Agency (IAEA) and U.N. Security Council (UNSC) actions
• Iran designated "state sponsor of terrorism."	1984	
	1985	
	1986	
• Executive Order 12613 – U.S. imports of Iranian goods banned.	1987	
	1988	
	1989	
	1990	
	1991	
• Iran - Iraq Arms Nonproliferation Act of 1992 – sanctions against foreign parties engaging in proliferation activities (advanced conventional weapons) that contribute to Iran's efforts in this area.	1992 1993 1994	
• Executive Order 12957 – restrictions on U.S. involvement with the development of Iran's petroleum resources.	1995	
• Iran-Libya Sanctions Act of 1996 (ILSA) – sanctions against parties that invest $40 million or more in the development of Iran's petroleum resources. After the first year, sanctions shall be applied to nationals of nonwaiver countries who invest $20 million or more.	1996	

(Continued).

U.S. government sanctions		International Atomic Energy Agency (IAEA) and U.N. Security Council (UNSC) actions
• Executive Order 13059 – consolidation of prior executive orders, prohibition on trade and investment activities with Iran.	1997	
	1998	
	1999	
• Iran Nonproliferation Act of 2000 – sanctions against foreign persons transferring controlled goods (nuclear, biological, or chemical weapons, or ballistic or cruise missile systems) to Iran.	2000	
	2001	
	2002	
	2003	•June: IAEA states that Iran failed to report certain nuclear materials and activities and requests cooperation from Iran.
	2004	• November: under the Paris Agreement with the European Union-3 (Britain, France, and Germany), Iran agrees to suspend enrichment in exchange for renewed trade talks and other aid.
• Iran Nonproliferation Amendments Act of 2005 – amended Iran Nonproliferation Act of 2000 to include Syria (renamed Iran and Syria Nonproliferation Act).	2005	• August: Iran breaks the seals on its uranium conversion facility at Isfahan; IAEA calls on Iran to suspend enrichment-related activities.
• Iran Freedom Support Act – amended ILSA to (1) add nuclear, chemical, biological, advanced conventional weapons as sanctionable, (2) remove Libya from ILSA (renamed Iran Sanctions Act).	2006	• January: Iran resumes enrichment activities. • February: IAEA votes for a resolution to report Iran to the UNSC. • July: UNSC resolution 1696 calls for Iran to suspend all uranium enrichment related and reprocessing activities.

(Continued).

U.S. government sanctions		International Atomic Energy Agency (IAEA) and U.N. Security Council (UNSC) actions
		• December: UNSC resolution 1737 requires Iran to suspend its uranium enrichment and reprocessing activities as requested under resolution 1696 and decides that all states take measures to prevent the supply, sales or transfer of all items, goods and technology, which could contribute to Iran's enrichment-related activities or the development of nuclear weapon delivery systems.
North Korea Nonproliferation Act of 2006 – amended Iran and Syria Nonproliferation Act to include North Korea (renamed Iran, North Korea, Syria Nonproliferation Act).		
	2007	•March: UNSC resolution 1747 requires Iran to suspend enrichment by May 2007. This resolution widened the scope of the previous resolution by banning Iran's arms exports and freezing the assets and restricting travel of additional individuals engaged in the country's proliferation-sensitive nuclear activities. • May: IAEA reports that Iran has not suspended its uranium enrichment activities and has continued operation of its pilot fuel enrichment plant.

Figure 3. Establishment of U.S. and UN Sanctions Targeting Iran.

Chapter 9

APPENDIX III: SANCTIONS IMPOSED UNDER THE LAW CURRENTLY KNOWN AS THE IRAN, NORTH KOREA, AND SYRIA NONPROLIFERATION ACT

Table 5. Imposition of Sanctions under the Iran Nonproliferation Act (INPA) and the Iran and Syria Nonproliferation Act (ISNA), 2001-2007, Iran-Related Cases[a]

Country of sanctioned parties	Number of sanctioned parties
Iran Nonproliferation Act of 2000	
Sanctions imposed against foreign parties from	
2001 to 2006	
China	46[b]
North Korea	9
India	6
Russia	5
Armenia	2
Moldova	2
Macedonia	2
Belarus	2
Taiwan	2
All others	5
Total	81
Iran and Syria Nonproliferation Act	
Sanctions imposed against foreign parties in 2006 to 2007	
Syria	8
China	6

Table 5. (Continued).

Country of sanctioned parties	Number of sanctioned parties
Sudan	3
Malaysia	3
Russia	2
Iraq	2
Mexico	2
Pakistan	2
All others	2
Total	30
Both Acts Combined	
Sanctions imposed against foreign parties, 2001 to	
2007	
China	52
North Korea	9
Syria	8
Russia	7
India	6
Malaysia	3
Sudan	3
All others	23
Total	111

Sources: http://www.state.gov/t/isn/c15231.htm, *Federal Register*.

[a] The Iran Nonproliferation Act of 2000 (INPA) was amended to include Syria in 2005 (the Iran and Syria Nonproliferation Act, or ISNA), and North Korea in 2006, and is now known as the Iran, North Korea, and Syria Nonproliferation Act (INKSNA).

[b] For the total number of sanctions involving parties from specific countries, in particular China, the total number of sanction cases includes multiple instances of sanctions that were imposed against the same party.

Chapter 10

APPENDIX IV: POTENTIAL INVESTORS IN IRAN'S ENERGY SECTOR

The following table illustrates various major agreements between Iran and foreign firms and governments in Iran's energy sector.[1] The table is not intended to imply a complete or thorough listing of foreign deals. Because several of these deals are in progress, we are making the conservative assumption that these agreements, at a minimum, express commercial interest between Iran and the foreign party to trade, finance or underwrite a project in Iran's energy sector.

Table 6. List of Recent Major Agreements between Iran and Foreign Investors in Iran's Energy Sector

Date	Type of agreement	Country/Investor	Type of investment	Amount	Status
March 2003	Binding Contract	France, Technip-Coflexip	Construction of an ethylene cracker on Kharg Island. (Petrochemical)	\$232 million	Completed
May 2003	Binding Contract	South Korea, Daelim	Engineering, Procurement and Construction (EPC) contract for 645,000 ton/year (t/y) capacity ethyl-benzene plant in Assaluyeh. (Petrochemical)	\$600 million	To be completed in 2008
January 2004	Binding Contract	Japan, INPEX	Development of the Azadegan oil field. (Oil)	\$4.45 billion	INPEX withdrew in 2006 from the project due to the political environment in Iran. National Iran Oil Company (NIOC) has since offered this project to domestic companies
April 2004	Binding Contract	Japan, consortium consisting of Japan's Toyo Engineering Corp. and Chiyoda Corp	Construction of a 670,000 t/y ammonia and urea plant in Assaluyeh. (Petrochemical)	\$220 million	To be completed in late 2007

Date	Type of agreement	Country/Investor	Type of investment	Amount	Status
August 2004	Binding Contract	Brazil, Petrobras	Exploration and Development Contract for the Tusan block. If commercial volumes of hydrocarbons are found, Petrobras will be awarded the contract for the development of the field(s). (Oil)	$34 million	Near completion
January 2005	Binding Contract	Consortium: South Korea, Daelim; UK's SembCorp Simon- Carves	EPC Contract for a 300,000 t/y LDPE at the Amir Kabir petrochemical plant. (Petrochemical)	$242 million	To be completed in 2008
March 2005	Binding Contract	Thailand, PTT Exploration and Production (PTTEP)	Exploration and development contract for the Saveh block. If commercial volumes of hydrocarbons are found, PTTEP will invest up to $39 million for further appraisals of the block. Upon completion of exploration for commercial hydrocarbon reserves, PTTEP will be awarded the contract for the development of the field(s). (Oil)	$5.4 million (Minimum exploration contract)	In progress

Table 6. (Continued).

Date	Type of agreement	Country/Investor	Type of investment	Amount	Status
May 2005	Binding Contract	China, China National Petroleum Corporation (CNPC)	Exploration and development contract for the Kuhdasht Block. If commercial volumes of hydrocarbons are found, CNPC will invest up to $51 million for further appraisals of the block. Upon completion of exploration for commercial hydrocarbon reserves, CNPC will be awarded the contract for the development of the field(s). (Oil/Gas)	$18 million (Minimum exploration contract)	In progress
July 2005	Binding Contract	Consortium: UK, Costain Oil, UK, Gas and Process; Spain, Dragados	EPC of Bid Blonad 2 gas processing plant. (Gas)	$1.42 billion	To be completed sometime in 2010-2011
July 2005	Binding Contract	Consortium: South Korea, Hyundai Engineering and Construction Co; German, Linde	EPC of a 1.2 million t/y ethylene plant. (Petrochemical)	$1.3 billion	To be completed sometime in 2009-2010
August 2005	Binding Contract	Italy, Tecnimont	Construction of a 300,000 t/y LDPE plant at Sanadaj (Kordestan). (Petrochemical)	$292 million	To be completed sometime in 2009-2010

Date	Type of agreement	Country/Investor	Type of investment	Amount	Status
November 2005	Binding Contract Binding Contract	Italy, Tecnimont Italy, Tecnimont	Construction of 300,000 t/y LLDPE/HDPE plant (Petrochemical). Construction of 30,000 t/y Butene-1 plant at Khorramabad (Lorestan). (Petrochemical)	Total contracts worth: $536 million	To be completed in 2010
November 2005	Binding Contract	Japan, Mitsui Engineering and Shipbuilding Co. (MES)	EPC contract for 300,000 t/y HDPE petrochemical plant in Ilam province. (Petrochemical)	$288 million	To be completed in 2010
May 2006	Binding Contract	German ABB Lummus	EPC contract for the expansion of Abadan oil refinery to increase gasoline production. (Oil refining)	$478 million	To be completed sometime in 2009-2010
June 2006	Binding Contract	China, China Petroleum and Chemical Corporation (Sinopec)	Exploration and development contract for the Garmsar Block. If commercial volumes of hydrocarbons are found, Sinopec will be awarded the contract for the development of field(s).	$19.6 million (Minimum investment)	In progress

Table 6. (Continued).

Date	Type of agreement	Country/Investor	Type of investment	Amount	Status
August 2006	Binding Contract	China, China Petroleum and Chemical Corporation (Sinopec)	Upgrade 8 existing units of the Arak refinery in the Markazi province and add 14 more units to increase gasoline production.	$1.6 billion	To be completed in 2010
September 2006	Binding Contract	Norway, Norsk Hydro ASA	Exploration and development contract for the Khorramabad Block. If commercial volumes of hydrocarbons are found, Norsk Hydro will invest up to $58 million for further appraisals of the block. Upon completion of exploration for commercial hydrocarbons reserves Norsk Hydro will be awarded the contract for the development of the field(s). (Oil)	$49 million (Minimum exploration contract)	In progress

Date	Type of agreement	Country/Investor	Type of investment	Amount	Status
October 2006	Binding Contract	Italy, IRASCO s.r.l, subsidiary of Iran International Engineering Company (IRITEC)	Kharg and Bahregansar associated gas gathering and Natural Gas Liquids (NGL) recovery project. (Kharg NGL project) (Natural Gas)	\$1.6 billion	To be completed in 2010
November 2006	Nonbinding Memorandum of Understanding (MOU)	Australia, Liquefied Natural Gas Limited (LNG Ltd)	Development of Salkh (Qeshm 4) and Southern Gashu gas fields and the construction of a 3.4 mtpa LNG plant (Qeshm LNG) on Qeshm Island. (Natural gas)	This is a preliminary agreement, no details available.	Under negotiations
November 2006	Binding Contract	Consortium: German, ABB Lummus	EPC Contract for increasing of gasoline production in Bandar Abbas oil refinery. (Oil refining)	\$442 million	To be completed in 2010
December 2006	Nonbinding MOU	China, China National Offshore Oil Corporation (CNOOC)	Development of the North Pars gas field for LNG Exports. (Natural Gas)	\$16 billion	Under negotiations
December 2006	Binding contract	China, Sinopec	EPC contract for gasoline production unit at Tabriz refinery. (Oil refining)	\$ 144.7 million	To be completed in 2009

Table 6. (Continued).

Date	Type of agreement	Country/Investor	Type of investment	Amount	Status
December 2006	Nonbinding MOU	Iran and Belarus (Inter government agreements)	Development of the Jofeir oil field. (Oil)	NIOC announced negotiations with Belarusian party is near completion and the contract is expected to be signed in July 2007.	Under negotiations
January 2007	Nonbinding MOU	Malaysia, SKS Ventures	Development of the Golshan and the Ferdos gas fields for LNG exports. (Natural Gas)	$16 billion	Under negotiations
February 2007	Nonbinding contract	Netherlands, Shell; Spain, Repsol	Development of Phases 13 and 14 (Persian LNG). Shell (25%), Repsol (25%). (Natural Gas)	$4.3 billion	Contract effectiveness is subject to Persian LNG final investment decision (FID). Start-up depends on project FID
February 2007	Binding contract	Korea, Daelim	Agreement on the construction of LNG and LPG storage tanks for the Iran LNG plant and the construction of port and dock facilities. (Natural Gas)	$500 million	To be completed in 2014-2015

Date	Type of agreement	Country/Investor	Type of investment	Amount	Status
March 2007	Binding contract	Consortium: South Korea, Daelim; German, Lurgi and UHDE	EPC contract for upgrading the Isfahan oil refinery. (Oil refining)	\$1.72 billion	To be completed in 2012
April 2007	Binding contract	Indonesia, Star Petrogas	EPC contract for Bandar Abbas condensate splitter. (Oil refining)	Approximate worth of contract at \$2 billion	To be completed in 2010
May 2007	Nonbinding Heads of Agreement (HOA)	Austria, OMV	OMV has 20% share in the development of South Pars Phase 12 and holds 10% share in Iran LNG Project. OMV also agreed to buy 2.2 mt LNG from Iran LNG Project. (Natural Gas)	Early planning stages, no details	Under negotiations
May 2007	Nonbinding MOU	Iran and Oman (inter government agreement)	Construction of a 670,000 t/y ammonia and urea plant in Assaluyeh. (Petrochemical)	This is a preliminary agreement, no details available.	Under negotiations
May 2007	Nonbinding MOU	Iran and Oman (inter government agreement)	Construction of a gas pipeline from Iran to Oman and the cooperation in LNG production and development of Hengam gas field. (Natural gas)	This is a preliminary agreement, no details available.	Under negotiations
May 2007	Nonbinding MOU	Iran and Iraq (inter government agreement)	Construction of an oil pipeline. (Oil infrastructure)	This is a preliminary agreement, no details available.	Under negotiations

Source: FACTS Global Energy

Note: Contract worth stated in this list only constitutes those contracts signed with foreign companies. For exploration and development contracts, the contract value (minimum-maximum range applies only for exploration activities. Should oil and gas reserves be found, new contracts for field development are required to be signed. Heads of Agreement (HOA) and Memoranda of Understanding (MOU) are not normally binding or completed deals. These are typically preliminary stage agreements with the intention to create a legally binding contract and are used to identify the principal elements of the deal. In general, typical preliminary stages can include Letter of Indication or Letter of Interest, MOU, Letter of Intent, HOA, and Confirmation of Intent. In the table, a binding contract means that it is a done deal and is legally binding. Nonbinding deals such as MOUs and HOAs and preliminary agreements and are generally beyond the stage of a Letter of Interest (i.e., expressed commercial interest to trade, finance or underwrite the project). We did not independently review the contracts.

REFERENCES

[1] The House Committee on Ways and Means defined "unilateral sanctions" as such in a February 18, 1998, letter to the U.S. International Trade Commission Chairman.

[2] Exec. Order No. 13059, 62 *Fed. Reg*. 44,531 (Aug. 19, 1997).

[3] See Exec. Order No. 13224, 66 *Fed. Reg*. 49,079 (Sept. 23, 2001); Exec. Order No. 13382, 70 *Fed. Reg*. 38,567 (June 28, 2005).

[4] We are reporting global trade data in constant 2006 dollars. This reflects the real value of Iran's trade. (See app. I for further explanation regarding the method used to adjust the nominal trade figures reported by the International Monetary Fund [IMF] into 2006 dollars).

[5] S.C. Res. 1737, U.N. SCOR, 61st Sess., U.N. Doc. S/RES/1737 (2006); S.C. Res. 1747, U.N. SCOR, 62nd Sess., U.N. Doc. S/RES/1747 (2007).

[6] A ban on imports of Iranian goods and services was enacted in October 1987 via Executive Order 12613, 52 *Fed. Reg*. 41940 (Oct. 29, 1987). In March 1995, the President issued Executive Order 12957, 60 *Fed. Reg*. 14615 (Mar. 15, 1995) prohibiting U.S. involvement with petroleum development in Iran. Executive Order 12959, 60 *Fed. Reg*. 24757 (May 6, 1995) was issued 2 months later, banning specified exports and investment. Finally, on August 19, 1997, the President signed Executive Order 13059, 62 *Fed. Reg*. 44531 (Aug. 19, 1997) which consolidated prior executive orders and prohibits virtually all trade and investment activities with Iran by U.S. persons, wherever located.

[7] Executive Order 13059 defines "U.S. persons" as "...any United States citizen, permanent resident alien, entity organized under the

laws of the United States (including foreign branches), or any person in the United States."

[8] Some U.S. companies have come under scrutiny for dealings by their foreign subsidiaries with Iran. For example, the U.S. company Halliburton announced in 2005 after criticism of a subsidiary's involvement with Iran that its subsidiaries had completed all contractual commitments with Iran and that it would no longer operate there.

[9] With some exceptions, the ban does prohibit foreign persons from reexporting sensitive U.S.-origin goods, technology, or services to Iran. Executive Order No. 13059, § 2(b). Sanctions were recently extended by the Department of Commerce's July 12, 2007, addition of five Iranian entities to the Entity List. All reexports of any item subject to the Export Administration Regulations now require an export license, with a presumption of denial, to the listed entities.

[10] See Iranian Transaction Regulations: Licensing of Imports of, and Dealings in, Certain Iranian-Origin Foodstuffs and Carpets, 65 *Fed. Reg.* 25,642 (May 3, 2000).

[11] Agriculture, Rural Development, Food and Drug Administration, and Related Agencies Appropriations Act, 2001, Pub. L. No. 106-387, Title IX, § 906, 114 Stat. 1549, 1549A-69 (2000). This law enacted as U.S. policy the principle that commercial sales of food, other agricultural products, medicine, and other medical products shall not be used as a tool to conduct foreign policy or to address national security objectives.

[12] Our previous work noted that sanctions can increase the costs of trade and finance to the sanctioning nation (in this case, the United States) because it loses commercial transactions and profits with the target nation. See GAO *Economic Sanctions: Effectiveness as Tools of Foreign Policy*, GAO/NSIAD-92-106 (Washington, D.C. Feb. 19, 1992).

[13] International Emergency Economic Powers Enhancement Act, Pub. L. No. 110-96, § 2, 121 Stat. 1011 (2007) (codified at 50 U.S.C. § 1705).

[14] The Iran Nonproliferation Act of 2000 (INPA) was amended to include Syria in 2005 (the Iran and Syria Nonproliferation Act, or ISNA), and North Korea in 2006, and is now known as the Iran, North Korea, and Syria Nonproliferation Act of 2006 (INKSNA), Pub. L. No. 106-178, 114 Stat. 38 (codified as amended at 50 U.S.C. § 1701 note).

[15] The act refers to controls established under numerous multilateral export control lists, including under the Australia Group, Chemical Weapons Convention, Missile Technology Control Regime, Nuclear Suppliers Group, and the Wassenaar Arrangement.

[16] The Department of State's International Security and Nonproliferation (ISN) Bureau was in charge of this effort until 2007 when the department's Verification, Compliance, and Implementation (VCI) Bureau took over this responsibility.

[17] Pub. L. No. 102-484 (codified as amended at 50 U.S.C. § 1701 note).

[18] The Iran-Iraq Arms Nonproliferation Act applies to Iran specific sanctions against Iraq as established in section 586G of the Iraq Sanctions Act of 1990, as contained in the Foreign Operations, Export Financing, and Related Programs Appropriations Act, 1991, Pub. L. No. 101-513, §§ 586-586J, 104 Stat. 1979, 2047-55 (1990). These sanctions include a prohibition on exports of items on the CCL, which falls within the Export Administration Regulations and establishes all items that are determined to have a potential "dual use" – that is, a use that has both a commercial and military or other strategic application. See 50 App. U.S.C. §§ 2401-2420; 15 C.F.R. Pt. 774, Supp. 1. Such exports to Iran can only be allowed if a presidential waiver is granted citing that a waiver is essential to the national interest of the United States. See Pub. L. No. 102-484, § 1606. State officials in the Economic, Energy and Business Bureau (EEB), the bureau responsible for coordinating this waiver process, report that such waivers are granted infrequently.

[19] For sanctions imposed under this act, we are unable to provide information that specifies which sanctions were due to proliferation activities with Iran and which were due to proliferation activities with Iraq. Such information is classified.

[20] Pub. L. No. 104-172. Libya was removed from the act in 2006 by the Iran Freedom Support Act, Pub. L. No. 109-293, and the act is now known as the Iran Sanctions Act.

[21] Waivers are available under this act if the President determines that a waiver is important to the U.S. national interest.

[22] For example, the report stated that Petronas had only limited connections to the United States and Total had divested many of its U.S. assets prior to entering into the South Pars contract.

[23] In addition to these financial sanctions, other broad sanction tools available for use against any violating party, including Iran, include

Executive Order 12938, which targets proliferation of WMD. Exec. Order No. 12938, 59 *Fed. Reg.* 58,099 (Nov. 14, 1994). Since 1998, this order has been used to impose sanctions against multiple parties that have engaged in proliferation activities related to Iran's nuclear or missile programs.

[24] Exec. Order No. 13382, 70 *Fed. Reg.* 38,567 (June 28, 2005).

[25] Exec. Order No. 13224, 66 *Fed. Reg.* 49,079 (Sept. 23, 2001).

[26] Pub. L. No. 95-233, Title II, 91 Stat. 1625 (1977) (codified at 50 U.S.C. § 1701 et seq). IEEPA grants certain authorities to the President to deal with unusual and extraordinary threats if the President declares a national emergency with respect to such threat. For example, under IEEPA, the President may prohibit transactions involving any property in which a foreign country or national thereof has any interest by any person subject to the jurisdiction of the United States.

[27] A U.S. person is defined as any United States citizen or national or permanent resident alien anywhere in the world; entity organized under the laws of the United States or any jurisdiction within the United States (including foreign branches); or any person in the United States.

[28] Treasury also posts information on its Web site and publishes designations in its Specially Designated Nationals (SDN) list. Treasury officials note that U.S. financial institutions use the SDN list to identify and freeze assets of sanctioned parties.

[29] The designated entities are Pars Tarash, Farayand Technique, Fajr Industries Group, and Mizan Machine Manufacturing Group.

[30] The IRGC is a component of Iran's military, focusing on national security, internal and border security, and law enforcement.

[31] While official data on U.S. investment in Iran are incomplete, available figures indicate negligible U.S. investment in Iran, even prior to the adoption of the investment ban in 1995.

[32] For example, according to the Department of Energy's Energy Information Administration (EIA), Iran utilizes buyback contracts, which are arrangements in which the contractor funds all investments, receives remuneration from the Iranian government in the form of an allocated production share, then transfers operation of the field to Iran after a set number of years, at which time the contract is completed. However, according to U.S. Iran country report, the buyback of 5 to 7 years has not given contractors sufficient time to recoup their investment costs. Also, according to a

State Department report, a number of other negative elements in addition to the relative difficulty of reaching satisfactory arrangements affect foreign investment in Iran: prohibitions on foreign ownership of natural resources, sometimes unappealing financial and other contractual terms, alleged corruption, and political uncertainty are among the other negative elements.

[33] A recent project by the American Enterprise Institute (AEI) cites 300 companies from 38 countries that, as of May 2007, have, at a minimum, expressed commercial interest to trade, finance, or underwrite a project in one of Iran's economic sectors.

[34] According to Department of Treasury sources, targeted financial measures are "directed specifically at individuals, key regime members, front companies, and financial institutions." Targeted financial measures are aimed at "conduct" not a country. Some of these targeted measures require financial institutions to freeze funds and close the accounts of designated actors, effectively denying these actors access to the traditional financial system.

[35] Additional Designation of Entities Pursuant to Executive Order 13382, 72 *Fed. Reg.* 7,919 (Feb. 21, 2007).

[36] Iranian Transaction Regulations, 71 *Fed. Reg.* 53,569 (Sept. 12, 2006).

[37] According to Treasury officials, states engaged in sanctionable activities have been subject to sanctions and export control restrictions for decades and have adopted a variety of evasive techniques.

[38] These seven banks are HSBC (UK), UBS (Switzerland), Barclays (UK), Société Général (France), ABN (Netherlands), Standard Chartered (UK), Deutsche Bank (Germany).

[39] An export credit is a loan to the buyer of an export, extended by the exporting firm when shipping the good prior to payment, or by a facility of the exporting country's government. In the latter case, by setting a low interest rate on such loans, a country can indirectly subsidize exports. An export credit guarantee is a government-sponsored credit guarantee for commercial financing of exports, often to protect a country's exporters against potential loss due to nonpayment by foreign buyers.

[40] According to a Treasury official, "Iran is one of the largest beneficiaries of official export credits and guarantees, with $22.3 billion in exposure reported by OECD countries as of the end of 2005." Exposure means that the countries that provided export credit

guarantees are now vulnerable, or responsible, for the payment should something go amiss with the exports, such as the foreign buyer not paying.

[41] In early 2006, the OECD raised Iran's risk rating, and the IMF reported in its 2007 Article IV consultation with Iran that Iran's sovereign debt was downgraded by Fitch due to perceived increase in country risk.

[42] Treasury also posts information on its Web site and publishes designations in its Specially Designated Nations list.

[43] The International Atomic Energy Agency (IAEA) is an independent agency affiliated with the UN established in 1957 to control and promote the use of atomic energy. Currently, the IAEA has safeguard agreements through the Treaty of the Non-Proliferation of Nuclear Weapons with more than 150 member states.

[44] In the Arak heavy water plant, heavy water is extracted from regular water by replacing the hydrogen atom with the deuterium isotope. It is used in certain types of nuclear reactors where plutonium is bred from natural uranium. Plutonium is used in nuclear weapons and for nuclear power production.

[45] GAO, International Affairs: Information on U.S. Agencies' Efforts to Address Islamic Extremism, GAO-05-852 (Washington, D.C.: Sept. 16, 2005).

[46] In 1984, the Secretary of State designated Iran as a state sponsor of terrorism for its repeated support for acts of international terrorism. The effects of this designation include restrictions on U.S. foreign assistance, a ban on defense exports and sales, certain controls over exports of dual-use items, and various financial restrictions.

[47] ILSA Extension Act of 2001, Pub. L. No. 107-24, § 3, 115 Stat. 199.

[48] We are reporting U.S. trade statistics from the Department of Commerce in 2006 dollars.

[49] Oil-related exports average approximately 80 percent of Iran's total exports.

[50] We are reporting global trade data in constant 2006 dollars. This reflects the real value of Iran's trade. (See app. I for further explanation regarding the method used to adjust the nominal trade figures reported by the IMF into 2006 dollars).

[51] Growth rates are calculated using ordinary least square, which takes into account the value of trade for each year over the designated time period, calculates the slope of the best fitting regression line, and

ensures that extreme changes in a single year do not give a distorted average growth rate for the period.

[52] In 1994, EU countries received one-third of Iran's exports and provided 50 percent of Iran's imports. At the same time, developing countries' share of trade with Iran has increased from 32 percent of Iran's exports in 1994 to 47 percent in 2006, and from 34 percent to 60 percent of Iran's imports over the same period, due in large part to growth of trade with China, India, Korea, and other Asian countries.

[53] GAO, *Sales of Sensitive Military Property to the Public*, GAO-07-929R (Washington, D.C.: July 6, 2007).

[54] CRS, *Iran: U.S. Concerns and Policy Responses*, RL32048, Ken Katzman (Washington, D.C.: June 2007).

[55] According to the *Oil and Gas Journal*, Russia has the largest reserves of natural gas in the world.

[56] Japan's and China's Iranian crude oil imports comprised 12.6 and 11.1 percent, respectively, of these countries' total crude oil imports in 2005. Also of note, Turkey, South Africa, Greece, and the Philippines obtained more than 25 percent of their crude oil imports from Iran.

[57] To assess the impact of future oil prices on the Iranian economy, the IMF and Iranian officials constructed a medium term budget and economic model. Assuming the agreed upon budget reforms will be implemented, the economy can achieve an annual average growth rate of 4.5 percent over the 2007-2008 to 2011-2012 period and a fully financed budget if average long-term oil prices are $65 per barrel. If long-term oil prices fall below $55 per barrel, the budget and implied growth rates would not be sustainable.

[58] According to one energy expert, Iran is in the midst of a major country-wide refinery expansion and upgrade program, and there is also a push to process more of its expected condensate supplies and at least partially reduce its gasoline dependence.

[59] Smart cards were introduced as a means to limit drivers' consumption of subsidized gasoline.

[60] According to economic experts and Iranian country authorities, Iran has experienced a rapid increase in non-oil exports in the last decade. More recently, however, Iran has taken steps to diversify and promote non-oil exports. According to academic researchers, non-oil exports as a percentage of total exports were just over 3 percent in 1979. In 2000, the last year for which data are available, non-oil

exports stood at almost 27 percent of total exports. In addition to petrochemical products, non-oil exports includes carpets, fresh and dried fruits, detergents and soaps, chemical products, ready-made clothes, metallic mineral ores, iron, and steel.

[61] Petrochemicals are a large group of chemicals derived from petroleum and natural gas, which are used for a variety of commercial purposes. The term petrochemicals refers to feedstocks–the chemicals used in petrochemical plants and the finished products made from feedstocks. Petrochemical products include common items such as plastics, soaps and detergents, solvents, fertilizers, rubbers, paints, drugs, rocket propellants, and synthetic fibers. Petrochemicals are also found in products as diverse as aspirin, luggage, surfboards, carpets, and phonograph records.

[62] S.C. Res. 1696, U.N. SCOR, 61st Sess., U.N. Doc. S/RES/1696 (2006).

[63] U.N. Doc. S/RES/1737.

[64] U.N. Doc. S/RES/1747.

[65] These six countries are the United States, the United Kingdom, France, China, Russia, and Germany.

APPENDIX I

[66] According to the IMF, data are collected from Iran's trade partners as well as from Iran. IMF staff use their best judgment to determine bilateral and global trade flows.

[67] According to the World Bank, during most of 1986 to 2006, Iran's official exchange rate did not reflect the actual market exchange rate (the official exchange rate and the market exchange rate do coincide beginning in 2003).

[68] These major trading countries include the G-5 countries (France, Germany, Japan, the United Kingdom, and the United States) through 2000. From 2001, these countries include the Euro Zone, Japan, the United Kingdom, and the United States.

[69] EIA calculates net export revenues as the weighted average spot price of Iranian crude oil multiplied by Iran's' net oil exports multiplied by number of days in the year. EIA calculates Iran's net oil exports as Iran's total liquids production (production of crude oil and condensates, natural gas plant liquids, and refinery processing gain or loss) less Iran's total petroleum consumption.

[70] EIA provided the reporting countries import statistics of their petroleum imports from Iran. These data are comparable to UN trade statistics data for the same 2-digit petroleum commodity breakdown, 2709.

APPENDIX IV

[71] All contracts are partner arrangements between Iran and the foreign party. However, we have not listed the Iranian partner. For example, both the first and second contracts are with National Iranian Petrochemical Company (NIPC). For the remaining contracts, other Iranian partners include, for example, National Iran Oil Company (NIOC), National Iranian Gas Company (NIGC), National Iranian Oil Refining and Distribution Company (NIORDC), among others. Also, consortiums are partnerships with Iranian companies.

INDEX

A

B

C

D

E

J

K

L

M

N

O

P

R

S

T